# Beyond the Rhine

Donald R. Burgett, age nineteen, photo was taken in Mourmelon-le-Petit after our return from Bastogne and Haguenau, Alsace, my third campaign and third wound. (author's collection)

# Beyond the Rhine

## A Screaming Eagle in Germany

Donald R. Burgett

★
PRESIDIO

Published by Presidio Press, Inc.
505 B San Marin Drive, Suite 160
Novato, CA 94945-1340

**Library of Congress Cataloging-in-Publication Data**

Burgett, Donald R. (Donald Robert), 1925–
    Beyond the Rhine : a Screaming Eagle in Germany / Donald
R. Burgett.
       p.   cm.
    ISBN 0-89141-697-8
    1. Burgett, Donald R. (Donald Robert), 1925– 2. World War,
1939–1945—Personal narratives, American. 3. World War,
1939–1945—Campaigns—Germany. 4. United States. Army.
Airborne Division, 101st—History—20th century. 5. Hitler,
Adolf, 1889–1945—Homes and haunts—Germany—Berchtes-
gaden Region. 6. World War, 1939–1945—Regimental histories—
United States I. Tilte.

D757 .B87 2001
940.54'1273—dc21

                        2001021553

*To my wonderful wife, Twyla, who has stood by me in all my endeavors for these past forty-nine years. To my sons, Kenneth, Mark, Gary, and Jeffrey and daughter René Burgett Powell. To all American military, men and women, of all generations who serve and have served to uphold the rights of all Americans and the American way of life.*

# Contents

# Acknowledgments

My thanks and gratitude for the gentle nudges to keep me going and the friendship that has developed between my editor E. J. McCarthy and me. Also for his suggestion for the title of this book, "Beyond the Rhine," when my creativeness failed.

My gratitude to Presidio Press for taking my writings on and doing a splendid job in producing quality work. My gratitude and thanks to Rhonda J. Winchell, my agent, who first saw and understood what I was trying to do, to tell the world of the patriotism and sacrifices of young American men and women who voluntarily stood and still stand in defense of their country and ours. And thank-you Rhonda for placing my works.

Again I must thank Jeffrey Reed, my neighbor, who took his time to guide me with my uncooperative computer. To Mark Bando, a fellow writer, friend, and help-person when I needed it. Thank-you one and all.

# Preface

During the 1930s rumbles, saber rattling, and fiery speeches by two dictators in Europe and an emperor in the Far East threatened the world with global war. In 1939 Hitler and Mussolini marched out to conquer and enslave the world. Europe called on the United States to enter the conflict on their behalf against the oppressors, but isolationism in America held strong to keep the United States out. "Europe is always at war, let them fight their own battles" was the general feeling. And for a time the United States did stay out.

On the other side of the world, Japan had been waging what appeared to be a successful campaign against China, until 7 December 1941, when Japan suddenly and deliberately attacked Pearl Harbor. America was in a war whether it wanted it or not. That attack was an atrocity not only against our government but against the American people; it bonded them as no other act could have possibly done. Americans not only called for victory, they cried for revenge.

Five days after that attack, with America still reeling from the serious blow it had received, Hitler and Mussolini declared war on the United States. Our country was thrown into a total world war, with or without consent.

It was because of this unspeakable Japanese atrocity that most young Americans, men and women, volunteered for the military; those too old were not accepted. Those too young, such as myself, had to wait until we were of age. On my eighteenth birthday, 5 April 1943, I volunteered for a newly founded branch of the army, the U.S. Paratroopers.

My older brother, Elmer, entered this service in the fall of 1942, as it was first formed and I followed into active military service 11 May 1943.

The training was brutal with only the toughest and most tenacious men making it all the way through to become full-fledged paratroopers. Many others failed during training to be washed out to other branches of service. The men who succeeded went on to make up an elite unit that could and would be dropped by parachute or glider behind enemy lines to seize and hold strategic priority targets, for the most part fighting against numerically superior and better armed forces. We became the American Airborne.

I became a trooper of the 101st Screaming Eagle Airborne Division, 506 Parachute Regiment, A Company. My comrades were the best "Uncle Sam" had to offer. We trained, fought, and played together until we became more than brothers; we became as one. We went alone behind enemy lines where others would not follow. We were to rely on each other and ourselves. As our regimental motto and crest "Currahee!" states, "Stand alone."

On our first combat mission into Normandy, we parachuted behind invasion beaches hours before the beach landings started, to cut assigned telephone and communication lines. We were ordered to liberate and hold the four bridges over the Carentan Causeway along with the river locks controlling the flooding of strategic areas. It was also our assignment to take and hold four roads leading from beaches to the inland. Without these roads in Allied hands, the men landing on the beaches would be stuck, stacking up and with no way off to be destroyed at the will of the enemy. Many other chores fell to our expertise including harassing and killing the enemy wherever we found them. All of our assignments were completed on or ahead of the time scheduled.

Prior to the Normandy Invasion, General Eisenhower was apprehensive of the airborne. After Normandy, General Ike was so impressed that he personally formed the First Allied Airborne Army, or the "First Triple A," as we called it. Within weeks of the victorious Normandy Invasion, General Ike assigned us, as members of the First Allied Airborne Army, to the command of Field Marshall Bernard Law Montgomery.

For seventy-two continuous days and nights under Monty's command we fought a close quarter's battle against superior forces of Germans who were well armed and backed by armor and artillery against our light infantry. We fought the total time in a battle that was lost in the first eight days under a command that refused to admit that his plan had failed and kept us in a war of attrition that all but destroyed our entire division. Still we gave it our best and did not yield one foot to the enemy. We liberated, secured, and held the objective assigned to us, "Hell's Highway," which ran from the south at Eindhoven to the Rhine River in the north across from Arnhem, where the British First Red Devil's Airborne Division and General Sosabowski's First Polish Airborne Brigade were destroyed as fighting units.

After the total failure of Operation Market Garden and finally, at General Eisenhower's command, Field Marshall Montgomery reluctantly allowed our battered American airborne division to leave Holland and return to France.

We had been out of Holland only three weeks when the German's big buildup and breakthrough shattered through the American lines in the Ardennes. The Battle of the Bulge had begun. At that time most of our crew-served weapons, machine guns, mortars, and bazookas were in ordnance for repair. Many of our men were without personal weapons, and some were under treatment for wounds and other maladies. Our ill-armed and -fed 101st Airborne Division manned by sick and wounded troopers and ranks filled with new replacements with little or no combat experience or training was rushed to Bastogne, to take and hold that city to the last man.

Bastogne, with its seven all important roads running through the center as the spokes of a wagon wheel, had to be taken by the Germans, or they would lose the war. The seven roads were the main lifelines of a vast moving panzer and panzer grenadier army in full attack. Fuel, troops, armor, ammunition, food, and medical supplies had to be transported over these main arteries.

By the same reasoning, we had to keep these same roads from the enemy's hands or the Allies would lose the battle and possibly the war. The temperature had dropped to an average of ten degrees below zero Fahrenheit. Our men were without proper weapons, ammunition, food, and winter clothing. Our field hospital surgeons and medical teams had all been overrun and captured the first night of battle; our severely wounded waited or died. In time many of our men suffered severe frostbite and later amputations.

In true paratrooper tradition, our one division with the aid of two-armored tank battalions, one tank destroyer platoon, and one battery of 155 Long Tom artillery manned by Negro troops stood off nine fully armed and armored panzer divisions for eight days. Given arms, ammunition, and winter clothing by troops that broke through our encirclement, we went into a frontal attack for an additional twenty-two continuous days and nights, until the enemy was fully beaten back to his own borders. These seven roads were hell for both sides, the Americans and the Germans.

The Germans' loss at the Battle of the Bulge, sealed their fate; they had lost the war. It was now a hare and hound chase by all troops in Europe to Berchtesgaden, the lair of Hitler and his henchmen who had withdrawn there; all the aforementioned has been related in first person in my previous memoirs.

The last days of battle contained within these pages are the crumbling decay of a super world ruled by a super race. There was no glory in the dust of defeat, only tidbits of worldly souvenirs to be gleaned by tired, ragged pursuers. There was no glory in the victory of war, only honor to those who fought bravely, and memories of those who suffered and died in battle. No one gave his life for his country; his life was taken from him. With these experiences, thoughts, and memories, I offer my legacy on printed page to whoever wishes to read it.

# 1 The Long Walk Out

We had fought well in the Battle for Bastogne—and we had paid a terrible price in lives of our comrades. We had been called up out of beds at 2:30 A.M., 17 December 1944, in our camp at Mourmelon-le-Grand, France. There the 101st Airborne Division packed, readied for battle, and were on the road in 380 open cattle trucks heading for Bastogne, Belgium, that same day. This was the first time in American military history that an entire division had been alerted and on the move toward combat in a matter of hours. It usually takes several weeks to ready a combat division for such a maneuver.

Upon arriving in Bastogne the division immediately went into action, attacking outward in all directions against far superior enemy armored forces. The 101st Airborne Division, without air support, held nine fully armed German divisions at bay for eight days and nights in subzero weather. We were aided only by a couple of battalions of the 9th and 10th Armored Divisions, one platoon of TDs of the 705th Tank Destroyer Battalion, and one battery of 155s manned by Negro artillerymen of the 969th Artillery Battalion. Ill armed, clothed, and fed, together we held Bastogne for eight freezing and grueling days. Patton's 4th Armored Division attacked at Assenfois, 26 December 1944, on our southern perimeter to breach the German lines surrounding us. We were then resupplied with weapons, ammunition, clothing, food, and a few new troop replacements.

Once we had received weapons, ammunition, food, and clothing we immediately went into an attack that lasted an additional twenty-two days and nights without a letup. After thirty continuous days of

battle our assigned mission had been accomplished. We had not only
stopped the Germans' advance, but we had driven them back to the
original lines of their jump-off attack in what was to become known
as "the Battle of the Bulge." It had all begun for us at 2:30 in the
morning on 17 December 1944. The end came at 9:10 P.M. on 17 January 1945.

Our battle for Bastogne was over. We had won. Fresh troops and
armor had finally moved up to replace us and relieve us of our burdens, and our tour of hell in the frozen Ardennes had come to an
end. For the last twenty-four hours the war had moved steadily on
without us and now seemed far away. We could scarcely hear the low
rumble of artillery in the distance as the Allies pushed the battle lines
ever closer to the German border. The Germans did not continue
the fight to gain or hold. They did, however, fight with vigor and determination and gave way slowly, grudgingly, to buy time to extract
their troops and war materiel out of the Ardennes and back to the
soil of the Fatherland, where each German would have good reason
to fight.

We bivouacked among our foxholes in a large snow-covered field
alongside a macadam road as we awaited orders. Large warming fires
were built without regard to telltale smoke that only the day before
would have invited incoming enemy artillery.

A truck convoy moving slowly came into view, then stopped in
place on the road when they saw us. Several drivers dismounted and
walked to us to identify our group. Once they were satisfied as to our
identity they returned to their trucks, drove them into our field, circling back to face toward the road, and stopped. Drivers and crews
dismounted, crawled into the backs of the trucks, and began throwing barracks bags, without much care or regard, over the tailgate and
sides of the truck into scattered piles on the ground. We were told
that these were our barracks bags and that we could go through them
to identify and retrieve our own.

As before, while we were in combat fighting for our lives, some rear
echelon had slit our bags open with knives and had looted everything
of value, even stealing the picture frames of loved ones. This left us
with nothing more than empty or near empty bags. Our clothes, jump
boots, uniforms, hard-won war souvenirs, and money had all been

stolen. Troopers protested to the truck crews, some to the point of accusing the SOS (Service of Supply) men of looting and theft and threatening to beat some of them. The SOS men nervously denied any knowledge of the theft and wasted no time in completing the unloading of their trucks and getting the hell out of the area.

Most of us left our looted and cut bags where they lay on the ground, returning in disgust to our foxhole area. Men sat around the fires in the snow and on their helmets, and while some began heating K-ration food on their trench knives, others began pulling off their boots—some of them for the first time in weeks—to see what was left of their feet.

I sat on the cold ground and unlaced my boots. They came off with some difficulty. My socks, what was left of them, looked like crud-encrusted spats, no toes or heels left in them. My feet had turned white as snow. Large cracks in the skin laced deep around them, and my toes were swollen. I washed them with slushy snow that had partially melted by the heat of the fire. While I was massaging my feet gently to bring back the blood circulation and warmth, some skin rubbed off. I had expected worse than that. I dried them thoroughly and pulled on some almost clean socks found in my looted bag and replaced my now dry boots. Many of the men's feet were in bad shape. Later, some men's toes, feet, or fingers had to be amputated.

General Maxwell D. Taylor had sent out a directive that all troopers be clean shaven, cleaned up, and looking their best before morning. So it was that later that afternoon, while we were sitting around the fires shaving, taking helmet baths, massaging our feet, scraping crud from our clothes with trench knives, and digging through what was left of our pillaged barracks bags, the 17th Airborne Division came marching up the road. The 17th troopers were fresh faced, well fed, clean shaven, and wore neat, clean jumpsuits.

Then we looked at ourselves. We had done our best, but our clothes were still somewhat dirty and ragged and we were gaunt and hollow-eyed, like we had been put through the mill. But we were full of spirit and began yelling friendly jibes at the newcomers, as is the custom with men of brother outfits. They responded in kind.

Some of the 17th Airborne troopers called back that they were here to relieve us and we'd better not get too damned smart or they wouldn't do it. It was difficult to believe. We thought immediately of hot showers, clean, warm bunks, clean uniforms, back pay, beer, wine, and women. And with most of us, in that order.

In reality, it was the 11th Armored Division, who had had their baptism of fire in the latter part of this battle and had, in those last days of the battle for Bastogne, fought alongside us to the end, who now relieved the 101st this day, 17 January 1945. The newly arrived 17th Airborne Division now moving up would be relieving the 11th Armored Division within the next few days.

Later that afternoon, as daylight waned and the air grew colder, our officers formed us up on the road to move out. The order of march was 3d Battalion, 1st Battalion, HQ, and 2d Battalion last, being relieved at 9:10 P.M. Moving into battle in Bastogne one month earlier, our order of march had been 1st Battalion, 3d Battalion, HQ, and 2d Battalion.

We were supposed to ride back to France in the same-style semi-trucks pulling open cattle trailers that had transported us to the front surrounding Bastogne. However, for some reason the motor transport division would not drive up to where we were. We would have to walk eight miles back to a monastery where the men of the motor transport sat waiting for us. *Monastery* may not be the correct term for the building we were to rendezvous at, but that is the way our orders read.

At convoy speed on icy roads the trip would have taken the trucks between fifteen and eighteen minutes to reach us from the monastery and about the same time to return with us as passengers. Carrying our weapons, ammo, heavy crew-served weapons, and seaborne rolls, that same trip on foot would take us approximately two and three-quarter hours one way.

The night became cold and dark as we shouldered our weapons and ammo and moved out down the road. We could no longer hear the big guns booming in the distance. Our mission had been accomplished. We were true to our word. We had held Bastogne from the enemy and we had defeated and beaten the Germans back to where they had come from. It had taken a lot more than the couple of days we had boasted it would—and a hell of a lot more fighting, suffering, and lives.

We marched in strung-out battle formation carrying our light and heavy weapons and newly acquired seaborne rolls, made up of what we had salvaged from our looted bags. The Sherman we'd found on the ridge overlooking Noville chugged along behind us like a huge, faithful mascot, bearing men on her back deck who were suffering too much pain to walk. They had done all the walking that was necessary. They had walked, run, carried their loads, and fought without complaint. Only now that the battle was over did they allow themselves the luxury of a short ride on the deck of a tank.

I looked at my buddies as we strode along. Their torn and ragged jump suits, though scraped with knives, were still dirty with grease. Sunken eyes glared watchfully out of gaunt, stress-lined faces. These men were soldiers? These men were paratroopers? These men were the elite "devils in baggy pants," the "butchers mit big pockets," who the Germans feared so much? Damn right they were.

I realized I looked no different than they. Strange, I hadn't really thought about it. I looked just as bad as the rest of them and I was damned proud of it.

It hurt to march tall and proud on cracked and swollen feet, but we did. We marched proud with frozen feet on frozen roads.

Again I heard the familiar sounds of the creaking of weapons straps and shoulder harness, the shuffling of jump boots on the snow-covered roads, and the muted clanks of machine guns, tripods, mortar tubes, and baseplates as they were shifted from shoulder to shoulder or from man to man. No one talked, each of us deep in his own thoughts. I thought of the truck ride from Camp Mourmelon-le-Grand, of the many men who were no longer with us—of Speer, Alvarado, Bielski, Horn, Chief, Barrington, and all the others. I had survived another operation. My seniority as an old man was growing. I was nineteen years old and now had three major campaigns under my belt. I had been wounded three different times and, in seniority, was one of the oldest of the old men. I had survived another one.

The temperature had dropped. We had no way of really knowing what the temperature was but felt it was again well below zero Fahrenheit. There was little wind, which was a blessing; if the wind had picked up, the cold would have cut through our clothing like a knife. The snow on the roads was packed hard as ice from the passing of American convoys heading toward the receding front. It made walking slippery, but the easiest we had experienced for weeks while trudging through snow chest deep—sweating all the while, then freezing when we stopped.

We marched at route step through the cold black night, maintaining combat formation as we went. The night became quiet, deathly quiet, no wind, no other moving troops, no traffic, no sound of small arms in pitched battles or the booming of artillery or the screaming of incoming shells to explode among us. The only sounds were the soft shuffle of our footfalls on hard-packed snow. The men were quiet, not talking. From time to time was heard the grunt or the cursing of a trooper as his foot slipped on the icy snow and he had to catch his footing and balance to keep from falling.

Our columns were shorter now, even with our replacements. It was only about eight miles back to the monastery where the trucks were waiting for us. We had walked into Bastogne on a dark, cold, quiet night, and now we were walking out. Eight miles through another dark, cold, quiet night. The distance didn't seem so far now. Hell, we had it made!

# 2 A Brief R and R

Our way to the monastery had been uneventful. We marched quietly, passing cadaverous burned-out German and American tanks, half-tracks, trucks, and other vehicles lining the side ditches where they had been pushed to clear the road for motorized and foot traffic. It seemed that wherever we went we left residue of battle, destruction, and death.

A shadowy image of a large building loomed before us, outlined against the lighter sky in the dark of night. Trucks and jeeps were parked in large numbers in the surrounding fields. A few vehicles, mostly command cars and officers' jeeps, were parked close to the main entrance on either side of the narrow road leading to and through the large open-gated main entrance. We entered through the archway and crossed an open, stone-floored courtyard, where we came to a halt and were ordered to fall out and find sleeping space. We spread out, searching through the buildings, some of them partially damaged by bombs or artillery.

In the dark we could see the forms of men wrapped in blankets, sleeping haphazardly in almost every room we looked into, on floors, on tables, or wherever. We moved to the far end of the courtyard away from the entrance, quietly entering a long, high-walled portion of the monastery, warily looking about. Approximately twelve wood-burning stoves ran back-to-back down through the center of the long, high-ceilinged room. They held fires, casting out golden rays of heat from small holes, cracks, and vents in the sides and tops. The floor was of concrete or smooth, close-fitting stone, swept clean.

No other troops were here, no persons were present or moving about. The huge kitchen was empty except for the stoves and cupboards. It did occur to us that the absence of troops sleeping or bivouacked here meant this room was off limits to enlisted personnel. But we were cold, hungry, and tired, so this was it. This was our place. This was where we would sleep. And we did, each trooper falling exhausted into place on the floor, head to foot, three and four abreast in front of the stoves. The unaccustomed warmth acted as a drug, and we slid into a dark sleep that came quickly. We dozed soundly, exhausted, secure in mind that we were far from the reaches of war and the enemy.

Something brushed past me. I awoke clutching my rifle that lay lengthways on my chest and belly. This was the way I always slept, my loaded rifle held close to my body front with finger on the trigger. For moments everything seemed strange. The snow, the woods, the sound of gunfire were gone. We were inside a building. Women dressed in black with starched white cowls moved about cooking. Others were busy carrying wood for the stoves or moving pots and kettles about. A middle-aged nun stood near me, busy at her chores. She moved closer, leaning toward the back of the stove. Again the edge of her floor-length skirt brushed my face. I sat up and looked about. Phillips, Justo, Liddle, Angelly, Benson, and most of the rest were already up. I was the lazy one, nearly the last one to awaken this morning of 18 January 1945.

We milled about a little, sneaking quick looks into the pots. It looked like oatmeal that was cooking. Finally one of our men got up the courage to ask one of the nuns if they might spare a little of their porridge. We didn't want to ask them for food, for we knew they had been on short rations for quite a while, but there seemed to be more cooking on the stove than what the nuns could possibly use and we were hungry.

One of the older women stepped forward. Speaking nearly perfect English, she explained that this food was not entirely for them, but more for unfortunate Belgians who had been left homeless or penniless by the war. Every day these people gathered in the cold at the monastery and lined up to receive what little the nuns could beg, borrow, prepare, and dole out. Our military in Belgium added quite a bit to their larder at this time.

We were hungry, too, and had neither rations nor any source of supply at the time. Finally groups of us wandered out to the court-yard. We could smell coffee and bacon on the morning air. It was tantalizing. We followed the sweet aroma to a GI kitchen set up in a wing of one of the buildings just to the right of the courtyard, as one entered from the archway. GIs of a motor transport company were lined up with mess kits, receiving helpings of pancakes, butter, syrup, bacon, and coffee. We asked the pudgy cook if we could join the chow line; it had been a long time since we'd had a decent meal.

"Hell no, I've got just enough rations to feed my own men. I can't feed every beggar that comes around."

Many of us had washed and shaved from our helmets with water from melted snow and scraped our clothing with knives at the fire the day before to look our best. We did remain a sunken-eyed, ragged-looking bunch, but we didn't think we looked or acted like beggars. We were hungry GIs without food, asking other GIs with food for a little bit to eat.

We walked out of the kitchen and sat on the cobblestones with our backs against the wall, trying to absorb as much of the morning sun as we could. We talked among ourselves. We decided to wait until the next group of noncombatants went into the kitchen for seconds and each of us would toss a live grenade in at the same time and get rid of the fat cook and the rest of his damned bunch.

A trooper strolled across the courtyard toward us, apparently eat-ing from his mess kit as he slowly walked in our direction. He stood in front of us, his mess kit filled with bacon, sausage, and buttered pancakes swimming in syrup, and his canteen cup filled with scald-ing coffee. "Where in hell did you get that?" one of our group asked.

"Over there on the other side of the courtyard," he replied. "There's a bunch of colored troops over in that bombed-out build-ing and they're feeding everybody that comes along."

We forgot about grenading the cook and his mess hall and ran for the colored kitchen, pulling our mess kits from our musette bags and leg cargo pockets at the same time.

Angelly, Phillips, Benson, Liddle, Sergeant Brininstool, and I, along with other troopers, were reluctant to cut into the chow line ahead of the other troops. We stood near the benches where the cooks ladled out the food, looking in awe at the amount and variety.

I felt like a hungry house-dog staring at a food-laden dining table while the masters ate.

The Negro troops stopped as if on command, smiled smiles that showed white teeth in dark faces, and told us to step right in and help ourselves. "Take all you want," they said. "There's plenty for everyone. We know you boys been fight'n and have missed quite a few meals. We can do without one if we have to."

We did as they asked, or insisted—we stepped in line and the cooks heaped breakfast on our mess kits till the kits just wouldn't hold any more. We thanked them heartily several times, and meant it. We walked back to the wall just outside the other kitchen and sat in the sunlight to eat our breakfast. We didn't wolf our food this time as had happened so may times in the past. This time we sopped each forkful of pancake in syrup and slowly chewed each bite of sausage and bacon, savoring it before swallowing. After a month of "fried snow" and K rations, this was a feast of feasts.

We finished eating and walked back to the colored kitchen, where we washed our mess kits and stayed on to talk at length with the colored troops. They were all interested in combat and asked us many questions about it. This was a unique experience for both of us, the colored and the white. Enforced segregation dictated that the two were kept separate, and these black troops were obliged to stay on their side of the courtyard and the whites stayed on their side, except on orders or when entering or leaving the main gate between them.

Again we thanked our hosts and returned to "our" side of the courtyard, where we took up positions sitting in the warm sunlight. That meal certainly took the wrinkles out of the belly. We discussed grenading the fat stingy, insulting cook in his kitchen, but with full bellies reasoning prevailed and we knew if we did, we would pay the price at a court-martial. We did watch him closely, however, and if he had stepped into a "quiet" part of the building's many nooks and corners, he would have paid a price. We no longer had the desire to do him in, but a good beating and a broken arm or leg would have been appropriate. I believe he noticed us watching him, and the look in our eyes, for he always managed to stay among several others of his men and never stepped into a vacant room or dark corner alone.

Our talk turned to the French towns we had visited before and of Paris and Reims and all the pretty young French girls who would be there waiting, just for us. *Vive la France.* We spoke randomly of thick steaks, cold beer, hunting and fishing, the old gang back home, and of mother, dad, and family.

In true army tradition we hurried, made ready to board the trucks, then waited. Orders were delayed, we didn't know why, for the trucks were parked outside and the drivers continued lounging in the monastery. We had been through this hurry-up-and-wait routine so many times that it didn't occur to us or enter our minds to wonder about it.

Later that afternoon of 18 January 1945 we were formed up under orders and loaded on six-by-six trucks instead of the larger, open-trailered semitrucks. We were driven approximately twelve miles south on the Bastogne–Neufchâteau Road to an area between Sibret and Bercheux, where we would be, until further notice, billeted in homes vacated by civilians under military order.

This same day, 18 January 1945, while we were in transit, divisional units and selected individuals of the 101st took part in ceremonies in Bastogne, honoring those chosen men with earned medals and the division as a whole for its gallant stand in Bastogne. I was never among those chosen to represent the division in any of these ceremonies and didn't feel neglected, but felt that men such as Ted Vetland, Sherwood "John Scott" Trotter, Charles "Red" Knight, James "Slick" Hoenscheidt, Joe Powers, Don Brininstool, Jack Bram, and several others should have been honored. It was they who were the leaders and the mainstay of Company A, 506th Parachute Regiment.

Gerald Day, our airborne tank driver, asked if I would like to be one of his crew on the way to our new billets. I accepted and climbed inside the Sherman. The convoy took off, and though we tried to keep up we were soon outdistanced and found ourselves making our way alone in the gathering dusk. Our latest company commander, twenty-year-old 1st Lt. William C. Kennedy, had foreseen this and had given us a map showing where we would be billeted until further orders. We should have no trouble finding the place.

I was sitting in the turret with a couple of other men as we sped on a long ice-covered downgrade of a hill. The sun had set and we were running with just our blackout lights on. Suddenly, through the dark, we could make out silhouette forms of tanks, trucks, and other armored vehicles in convoy crossing our front at the intersection at the bottom of the hill. Day hit the brakes, but our tank, not being fitted with cleats for the winter, skidded on its rubber pads, not seeming to slow down at all.

We slid toward the left of the road, which was lined with a deep ditch and huge trees. Our tank struck head-on against one of the trees and came to a sudden and jarring halt. The tank's left track was on one side of the trunk, our main gun tube was on the other. The big 76mm gun had gouged a large chunk of bark and wood from the tree.

We were lucky that we hit the tree and stopped as we did, or we would have ended up stuck in the ditch. The jolt of the sudden stop threw all of us from the turret into the driver's area. Someone, I don't recall who, had a busted lip and came up spitting blood, nothing serious.

Day managed to get our tank back onto the road. We recradled the 76mm gun, secured it in the barrel cradle, then continued on after the last armored vehicle in the convoy on the road below had passed by. We arrived at the designated farmhouse some time after the rest of the company, parked the tank next to the house that billeted 2d Platoon, A Company, picked up our seaborne rolls and weapons, and went in. Being the last to arrive, we had to take what was left of the sleeping areas. It is an unwritten law in the military among enlisted men, First come, first served, and all the choice sleeping spots had been taken.

The farmhouse was clean, furnished, and vacant. Inside we built wood fires in the stoves, received K rations, then set about cleaning weapons while we ate. After cleaning the weapons we began heating helmets of water to shave and take baths with. Men were too occupied washing socks, underwear, and other clothing to ponder on what might be in store for us in the near future. We naturally thought that after a month of combat in Normandy, seventy-two continuous combat days in Holland, and thirty continuous combat days in Bastogne, we had earned a rest and now would be sent back to France, with furloughs and passes to Paris and other cities. We talked of getting our back pay, and the wine, women, and other pleasures that awaited us.

Later that night we were a different-looking group. We were bathed and shaved. Our jump suits had been washed by hand and mended with needle and thread from our packs and cloth materials found in the houses. Some of the troopers brought out bottles of cognac they had "liberated" from hiding places where the civilians had secreted them. Belgians and French later remarked that the Germans couldn't find their cognac in four years of occupation. The Americans found it all in four hours. At least that is what they said. I believe a certain amount was left in not-too-secure hiding places for us to "find" and "liberate." That way we would be satisfied and the bulk of their "good stuff" would remain securely hidden, as it had been during the past German occupation years.

With oil lamps burning, the wood stove glowing, and the house and ourselves clean and comfortable, we passed the bottles around and made our toast, "Here's to the last one. Here's to the next one. Here's to the ones we left behind." Then we joined together in singing.

The night air was still and quiet. A light snow sifted down. It was a nostalgic night, the troopers were as one family. Our little "band combo" got together, as they usually did in such cases. Stratiff, playing his harmonica. Dobrich humming on a paper-covered comb. Another trooper played an assortment of pots and pans with a trench knife and wooden spoon. Vetland, holding a broom upside down and rubbing the butt end of the wood handle in short strokes across the grain of the wood floor, produced a rhythmic sound that closely imitated a bass.

Some of the songs we sang were "Begin the Beguine," "White Christmas," and the popular German song "Lili Marlene." Each time we sang "Lili Marlene" (the favorite of friend and foe alike in World War II) all joined in, but no two men ever sang the same words. No one really knew the correct words. But sing it we did, with all the feeling we could muster. Some of the troopers were recleaning their weapons, especially the machine guns. Our weapons were our lives; they came first.

Unknown to us at this time, an urgent call came from Seventh Army. The Germans had mounted another drive in force, "Operation Nordwind," which jumped off 1 January 1945, this time into the Alsace area, in an attempt to recapture Strasbourg and to isolate and destroy the Allied armies, one at a time. Again, our expertise would be needed in turning, containing, and defeating a German thrust. Advance parties of the 101st Airborne Division departed at once, 19 January 1945, to scout and appraise the situation. They arrived on the scene in Alsace on 20 January 1945. Major Leo H. Schweiter, temporary 101st Division G-2, studied VI Corps war maps and the situation and asked, "What the hell are you so worried about? The 101st alone can lick five German divisions simultaneously—we just did."

The nineteenth was our last day of R and R in the small vacated village and we spent it washing and bathing every chance we got and recleaning our weapons. We washed our clothes and ourselves in our helmets, while a few took turns bathing in a large galvanized washtub on the kitchen floor in front of the wood-burning stove.

The next day, around noon, a small convoy of semitrucks with long, open cattle trailers pulled into our area. The temperature was dropping; it was snowing heavily with small, hard granules, and the wind had increased. Troopers from surrounding houses walked in separate groups to the road, and without briefing or fanfare we loaded up with our weapons, ammo, gear, and rolls.

There was only one slight delay: a lieutenant had contracted diarrhea and fell victim to a personal accident. Our convoy waited while he stripped off naked in the subzero, wind-driven snow and, standing barefoot in ankle-deep snow, threw his long underwear away and redressed. Troopers all up and down the line whistled and whooped at his nakedness. All he could do was grin and bear it. He climbed shivering and blue-lipped aboard the truck, and the convoy moved out. We moved to the divisional area to link up with the rest of the convoy, to total approximately 110 ten-ton semitrucks with open trailers and nearly 100 six-by-six two-and-a-half-ton trucks with canvas coverings over the rear bed.

Under command of the convoy commander we moved out, each truck waiting until the one in front of it traveled the required distance before following. Maintaining proper distance between vehicles was important at all times in case of air attack or roadside ambush.

Silent troopers, each with his own thoughts, gazed at the rolling countryside. The roads were slippery; a cutting snow driven by harsh winds lashed our convoy. The temperature had dropped well below minus ten degrees Fahrenheit. The weather was as cold and bitter as any of the worst days we had experienced during the entire battle for Bastogne. No straw had been issued to insulate the trailer's steel floor, and we lay huddled close together in the long, open trailers to seek as much protection as possible. There was no chance for body heat to accumulate on the bare steel floor, even though we covered ourselves with the blanket each of us carried in our roll.

A man can lie for just so long, then he must stand and move his limbs as much as possible to keep circulation going in his body. Hour after hour went by, we rolled along with nothing but cold metal to lie or stand on in subzero temperature. When we stood, we were even more exposed to the frigid elements and the wind that slashed at us from overhead of the topless trailer. The steel floor transferred the cold through our boots until we could no longer feel our feet, only pain, then numbness. Pigs transported to the slaughterhouse receive better consideration.

We saw no recent evidence of war here, like burned-out tanks or smashed vehicles. All had been removed. I wondered, who did the clean up? It had to be the Americans. Holland, Belgium, or France at this time did not have the equipment to remove heavy wrecked war machines, like tanks and half-tracks. No longer did we think of enemy tanks, troops, or the Luftwaffe, even though the convoy ran with blackout lights. We thought only that we had survived another one and were now on our way back out of this mess to have a little R and R.

We managed to stand off the chilling weather with thoughts of arriving back at Mourmelon-le-Grand and receiving back pay and long passes to Reims and Paris. Each hour that passed, and each mile that fell behind, put us ever closer to warm barracks, hot food, and good times. We could handle the field problems, the chickenshit army routine, and the barracks life afterward. These thoughts, cradled in our brains, sustained us as we stood or lay as ice-encrusted zombies in the open trailers moving southward.

Our convoy, a long, slow, crawling anaconda of semitrucks, slid, skidded, and plowed its way through heavy gathering snows and piling drifts on slippery roads. Mile by mile Bastogne and the terrible

frozen war fell farther and farther behind. My thoughts drifted back
to the battles, blood-spattered snow, enemy dead, our comrades
killed, the heavy smells of battle and cordite. I felt comfort in the
thought that our Graves Registration Teams had arrived and our
comrades no longer lay dead, frozen, and abandoned in snow-swept
fields and cold, dark forests. They had been recovered, identified,
and buried in cemeteries, old and new. At least they were at rest until they would be moved again to larger American Memorial Gardens,
where they would rest with other comrades forever.

We headed southward, supposedly bound the way we had come,
through Neufchâteau, Sedan, and Verdun; then we were to head
westward, back to Mourmelon-le-Grand. But since the Bulge a "German attack" epidemic had spread throughout the western front. The
military was jittery, envisioning enemy breakthroughs everywhere in
their lines. Many army units sent out urgent distress calls, asking for
the immediate aid of the seasoned troops of the 101st Airborne to
stand on line with them against these threats. So in answer to the
frantic call from VI Corps Headquarters, the 101st Airborne Division
was ordered to move to an area threatened by the new German drive,
Operation Nordwind. On arrival we were to help bring the situation
under control.

Night came on. We lost track of where we were traveling, since we
could no longer see the road and town signs. We were totally unaware
of the new German offensive that had steamrollered 1 January 1945
into Alsace, in places breaking through American lines. American
forces were being driven back from the lines and those that stayed,
though they fought bravely, were also being forced slowly back and
in a nervous mood, possibly ready to be stampeded as had happened
in the Ardennes.

There was to be no rest for the weary. Our convoy, after leaving
Bastogne, Sibret, and Vaux-les-Rosières behind, did pass through
Neufchâteau as planned but then changed course. Our drivers
turned to follow their lead vehicles southeast to Bellefontaine, then
south through Vertun, Etain, and Toul, turning east through Nancy,
heading toward Haguenau in Alsace, near the German border and
the new German threat.

Before reaching the city of Haguenau the convoy came to a stop
alongside the road at Wickersheim. In the darkest part of the night

of 21–22 January 1945, men of the 101st Airborne Division de-trucked. It had taken our convoy thirty-six hours to travel 160 miles over icy roads, through strong winds, driving snow, and heavy drifts, to our destination. Cold, stiff, coated with ice, and tired from lack of sleep, we were briefed on Operation Nordwind and the German breakthrough in this area. There would be no rest for us; we would have to help hold the infantry's lines. There must not be another Bastogne, another "Bulge."

Regiments, battalions, and companies were assigned sectors. Men of Company A, 506th Regiment, shouldered machine guns, tripods, mortars, baseplates, and bazookas, picked up our ammo, and moved out on foot to bivouac in what was considered a quieter part of the lines between Sarrebourg and Dulingen. Here we were to relieve the 141st Regimental Combat Team of the 36th Division in the lines. We were now officially attached to the Seventh Army under overall command of Gen. Jacob L. Devers.

With this attachment of the 101st to the Seventh Army, the 101st became the only U.S. division ever to serve in three different army groups, in three different group combat areas, under three different commanding generals, all within sixty days. The 101st served in Holland under Field Marshal Bernard L. Montgomery, in the Ardennes under Gen. Omar Bradley, and now, in Alsace, under command of Gen. Jacob L. Devers.

Just before dusk we marched at route step in combat formation into the small village of Wickersheim. Our present company commander, 1st Lt. Bill Kennedy, told us to find billets for ourselves but not to get too comfortable—we could move out again any minute. My squad walked down what must have been the main street bordering one side of the town square, looking for a suitable place to sleep. We came to a building with a large glass window (rare in wartime Europe) fronting the street. Inside, standing on end and lying on sawhorses, were a number of plain varnished pine coffins.

We all had the same idea at the same time and the whole squad made a dash for the door. Inside we picked coffins for ourselves, spread the blanket from our seaborne rolls inside them, and lay down to get what sleep we could.

The coffins didn't make as good beds as we thought they would. They were too narrow, especially at the tapered foot, and confined the person lying in them. Then we saw Lieutenant Kennedy walking alone down the street in our direction. We lay still with arms crossed, with the serene look of undertaker-processed corpses. When Lieutenant Kennedy saw us, his mouth dropped open in shock. He came running through the door with .45 in hand and we all broke up laughing. He said that when he saw us he thought that some Alsatian Nazi collaborators had killed us and had put us on display as a warning to other Americans. All was forgiven and we slept inside on the floor, dry and out of the wind and snow.

The next few days were spent in relative quiet. The squads were then billeted in homes with civilians, most of whom did their best to make our stay comfortable. Over the years Alsace had been owned and ruled alternately by France and Germany. There were supposed to be approximately an equal number of French and Germans living here of their own will—whereas in fact, the larger portion of Alsatians were pro-German and pro-Nazi, not to be trusted. All people living here spoke both languages equally well, the predominant language being German. The residents who were pro-German kept their true allegiance secret, so they might strike harm whenever they thought they could get away with it. Some good but careless Americans died as a result.

One did not know whom to trust, a Frenchman speaking German, or a German speaking French. So we trusted no one. The plump older lady we stayed with brought out schnapps every night and stayed right with us drink for drink. We also shared what cognac or schnapps we had.

In our nightly talks we learned the Alsatian lady had one pro-Nazi son who had volunteered to fight with the German army and was still alive as of a couple of weeks before our arrival. The younger son had slipped away during the German occupation, made his way to England, and was somewhere fighting with the Allies; she didn't know exactly where or with whom, the English or the Americans. Nightly she prayed the two would never meet in combat. She feared that more than she feared them not returning.

We listened to "Axis Sally" on a small radio and joined in singing the American songs she played on her propaganda program. "Mama," as some of the troopers came to call her, would bring the radio out from a hidden place in the wall each night, returning it, out of habit, to hiding after we had all gone to sleep. She told us the Germans would have killed her and the entire family had they discovered the radio.

We wondered what ever happened to "Lord Haw Haw," the English traitor who at the outbreak of World War II had gone to Germany to preach propaganda over the wireless for the Germans. We hadn't heard from him lately. Perhaps the Germans had tired of him and had hanged or shot him. Both Lord Haw Haw and Axis Sally's efforts to demoralize the Allied troops by broadcasting news from home—reports on individual Americans, using their real names and their units—had the opposite effect. We looked forward to their broadcasts, their bits of news, the American music, and their boasts of the Third Reich winning the war.

We sat as a group with the old lady and her attractive young daughter in the small living room drinking schnapps and cognac and singing "Lili Marlene." Over and over we'd sing "Lili Marlene." The more we'd drink, the more we'd sing. The more we'd sing, the more we'd drink.

Earl Borchers, who had recently rejoined us after being severely wounded in Holland, sat soaking an injured foot in a pan containing a mixture of schnapps and hot water the old lady had prepared for him. She claimed schnapps would cure anything, inside or out, including minor sprains.

Her young daughter joined with us as a group but had to stay close under the watchful eye of her mother. Judging from her actions she would rather not have been under the close watchful eye of her mother. Most of the troopers tried to get next to her, but as far as I know, none succeeded.

# 3 Wickersheim

The German threat that had been expected in this area by Gen. Jacob L. Devers's Sixth Army Command did not materialize; we were no longer needed here. Again we received orders to move to another threatened area in the path of Operation Nordwind. The following day we were to begin our move, this time closer to the border of Germany.

We checked and shouldered our personal and crew-served weapons, gathered our ammo, backpacks, and seaborne rolls, bid the old lady and her daughter farewell, and thanked them for their hospitality. They stood together in front of their home with tears in their eyes. I knew the old lady was thinking of her own two sons as she watched us depart. Each of us left them a little something from our rations, a bit of candy, a few cigarettes, chewing gum, and several unopened boxes of K rations.

We were reenacting the very steps that had led us to the bloody "Battle for Bastogne," except this time we had weapons and ammunition. This time I didn't hear anyone talking of the souvenirs they would like to pick up. This time we wouldn't underestimate the Krauts. They were one tough bunch of military, but we had no doubt that we would kick their butts again. We still had our airborne tank with us, running on gas "appropriated" from the infantry's supplies. Gerald Day, an equipment operator in civilian life, was appointed permanent driver.

Smaller six-by-six, two-and-a-half-ton trucks entered our area to transport us to our destination in the vicinity of Hochfelden and Haguenau, some twenty-five miles away. The six-by-six trucks were smaller than the semitrucks we had moved in the last two times. The six-by-six trucks had protective coverings over the rear bed, with wooden side benches to sit on. Without briefing or fanfare we loaded up with our weapons, ammo, gear, and rolls. Again we moved out, with each truck awaiting its proper place in line. There was still no straw on the floor to guard against the cold, but we figured we didn't have far to go. It couldn't get much worse than what we had been through. This time, at least, we did have canvas covers to help ward off the winter wind and the ice and snow.

Men sat on the benches facing each other toward the center. A few sat on the floor up front while a couple sat on the floor near the tailgate. There wasn't enough room to really get comfortable, even with our diminished numbers. The command just cut down on the number of trucks required.

Again time and miles slid slowly by. We lost sense of distance, time, and direction. It really didn't matter—all that was real was the fact that once more we were going in, and somehow we all knew it would be a long, long time before we would rest again. Our hopes and dreams of passes and furloughs to Reims and Paris became an elusive will-o'-the-wisp.

Germany was near its end, and it was certain that all combat troops would be used constantly till the very end so the enemy wouldn't be given the chance to catch his breath. Just think of all that back pay we had coming, think of all the pretty little ma'amselles that were waiting, just for us. It would be a shame to be killed now.

Company A detrucked in the small town of Wickersheim, a calendar picture of one of those medieval Bavarian-style places that we were all too familiar with by now. The houses, buildings, and sheds were built so closely together, it seemed as though the outer structures pressed toward the center of town, forcing the inner buildings to rise up with larger protruding second or more floors that leaned out to each other over the narrow, haphazard streets. Huge dark wood beams formed geometric designs in the stucco outer walls. Narrow balconies protruded from upper fronts, further closing in over the streets below.

One farm building in particular where we detrucked on the outer edge of town struck me as a perfect country-style Bavarian home-

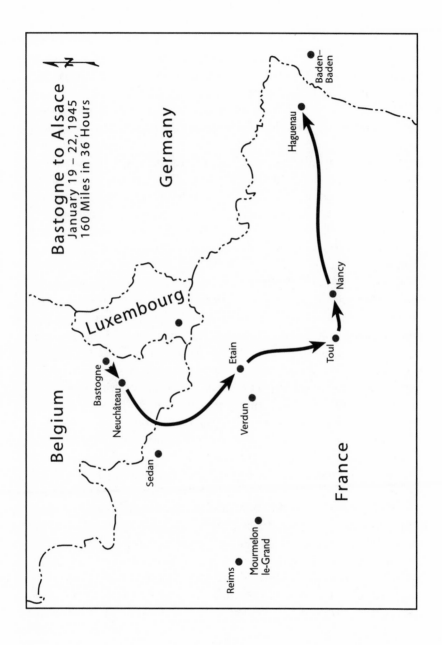

Bastogne to Alsace
January 19 – 22, 1945
160 Miles in 36 Hours

stead. A stone farmyard fence ran left along the roadside from the left side of the building as we faced it. A long stone barn running parallel to the road enclosed the far back of the yard. It was connected on the right end at right angles to the back of the house by a number of various-sized stone sheds that seemed to have been built one to the other as they were needed, forming a sort of wall, to include the house. Other buildings and connecting stone revetments at the far left end completed the enclosed bastion court of a small farm fortress.

Most of these buildings had been built several hundred years before to hold families, their livestock, and food stores, and indeed were constructed on purpose to form a fortress against marauding tribes or bands of transients who must have roamed this area at one time. Fascinated, I studied every foot of this structure as we stood outside awaiting orders. There were no sounds of battle, near or far. The night was unnaturally quiet.

A few GIs of the 222d Regiment, 42d Infantry Division who were billeted in the town hovered nearby in the road ahead talking among themselves. They were of a unit newly arrived from the States. Finally some of them approached warily, one of them asking apprehensively if we were the troops who were supposed to relieve them.

Our shoulder patches had been covered over with tape or a loosely stitched piece of cloth to conceal our identity, as was the custom when we were in transit. All divisional identification had been obliterated on all vehicles and mobile equipment, that we might not be recognized as the 101st "Screaming Eagles."

"No," answered one of our men, "we were just sent up here to help out."

The infantryman could not conceal his disappointment, but a second thought must have crossed his mind and he figured us to be green troops, replacements, and began telling us how rough the situation was in this area. A German patrol had entered the outskirts of this town the night before, 24–25 January 1945. They attacked an outpost, shot up a company of infantry, and captured an entire platoon of men with no apparent sign of a struggle, taking them back across the Moder River.

"But don't worry, " the foot soldier added, "we've been in tighter spots than this before."

"You don't say," replied Jack Thomas. "It makes me feel better knowing that you guys are here."

The infantrymen talked in low voices as they walked slowly back to a group of their comrades waiting for them near some vehicles parked farther down the road.

"They've been in rougher spots than this," one of our group said. "Wonder what they'd have done if they'd been in Bastogne with us?"

Sergeant Vetland returned from a briefing of noncoms and officers. "Follow me," he ordered, and led us into a large house farther down the road. This house and the rest of the town had been virtually untouched by the war; all appeared in good shape. "This is where the Second Platoon will spend the night."

The house had clean, spacious, vacant rooms, no furniture at all. Beautiful wood floors with carved wood trim throughout. A large glazed-tile wood-burning stove dominated the main living room, which contained sleeping closets with flush sliding doors built into the walls at either end. Squads spread throughout the house, choosing rooms as their own. A man picked his sleeping place in a room by dropping his musette bag and roll on the floor. This spot was uncontested as his from that moment on. Warm, clean, and out of the weather, with troopers of the 101st and men of the 42d Division on guard outside, we should get a good night's sleep for a change.

"Second Squad," Vetland called. We gathered around him. Tracing with his finger on a map under a flashlight, he described for us a route down the main street to a certain small road just out of town. We were to follow that road toward the enemy lines and set up an outpost in the farthest building on the left. This would be the same outpost the Germans had attacked last night, capturing an entire platoon of infantry.

We picked up our weapons, machine gun, ammo, and rolls and moved out in combat squad formation through the dark of night down the town's main road and past the sentries, after challenge and password, and beyond the far edge of town. One becomes accustomed to seeing in the dark, and after a short walk we came to the road running off to our right toward the enemy lines. Spread out in combat patrol with one man out front a scant hundred yards, we walked quietly down the rutty dirt road to our right toward the outpost.

Our two-track road sloped downward, leading past several small houses on either side that appeared to be vacant, abandoned temporarily by the owners in the face of an apparent oncoming battle. We stayed quiet, walking slowly with more distance trailing between men, staring into pitch-black darkness, listening intently. Each step could erupt in sudden shattering warfare. The infantry had pulled out of this area the previous night and back to town in the face of the enemy attack, leaving this entire front unattended except for possible enemy that could have filled the vacuum.

Slowly we made our way toward the enemy, each step of each man placed with care, each finger on the trigger, ears listening, eyes straining in a night that had become totally black. Then it was there, within a few feet of us, before we saw it—the house that was to be our outpost.

As the night darkened we had automatically closed ranks, getting closer and closer to each other so as not to lose contact. Not a wise move, but human nature prevailed without our realizing it. In our closed group we put our heads together and whispered a plan. We moved out, three men to the right, three men to the left, to make a radius sweep as wide as possible to make sure there were no enemy or booby traps around our outpost. I was with two others as we made our sweep toward the enemy and around to our left, then back to the outpost from the rear. Justo Correa and two others took the circuit to the right. The balance of the squad spread out in a semicircle at the front of the house as reserve, to give fire support in case of trouble and a base for us to fall back on if we needed to withdraw.

With our reserve spread out in a defensive perimeter, the rest of us, on returning from our patrolling action, carefully entered the house. After a brief inspection we signaled that it was okay for the rest to enter. We left the machine gun with three men outside as cover while we felt our way across the floor, sliding our feet slowly, tenderly, in a feeling manner. There was a lot of debris and litter on the floor, even a few weapons, but the place was evidently safe.

We set about covering the windows and door with blankets from our rolls as the three men with the machine gun began digging in.

One trooper held a flashlight covered with his hands so only the tiniest ray of light slivered between his fingers. He played this tiny light around the edges of the covered openings after two troopers had gone outside to look for any telltale light that might escape through an overlooked crack or small opening.

The two troopers outside covered the windows one at a time and themselves with a blanket while they checked for any hint of light from the inside. All windows and doors were checked in this manner, and after a little patching here and there the outside men announced that we were completely blacked out and stepped back inside. It was now okay to light the small oil lamp that Carl Angelly always carried with him attached to the back of his cartridge belt. Angelly had liberated the oil lamp from some barn in our recent travels, a miniature of the same-style metal-framed kerosene lamp our farmers in the States use in their farmyard work. In the light of the lamp we thoroughly acquainted ourselves with every inch of the building, rechecked for booby traps, then doused the light. We had to remain in total darkness to accustom our eyes in case of an attack. If an attack did occur and we had to extinguish a light or rush into the darkness from a lighted room, it would take several minutes to adjust our eyes to the darkness. In a shoot-out this would probably prove fatal.

We finished digging in the machine gun in a foxhole outside, just under the large front window commanding a broad view of the sector between the enemy and us. Three men stood watch on the gun outside, while others stood watch inside through peepholes in the blackout at the other windows. The rest of the men would sleep the best they could. Every two hours we would rotate the watches. Every man had a turn outside, inside, and sleeping. This being the twenty-sixth of January, it was still cold. Icy snow covered the ground and we could not build a fire inside for warmth. The smell of woodsmoke would certainly alert an enemy in the area that there was someone inside, and we would face an attack or a heavy shelling. At least we had overcoats and were inside out of the wind.

Morning came. We removed our blanket window-coverings just before daylight, so the enemy wouldn't see them. We had not seen or heard any sign of the enemy at all. We had wished the Krauts would show up so they would get their just deserts at the hands of experienced combat men.

With the blankets removed from the windows and door, light soon filled the place as daylight came. The sight that met our eyes was even worse than what we had been able to see with the light of our little oil lamp. American weapons were scattered about, rifles, BARs, bayonets, and a machine gun. Two Thompson submachine guns leaned against one of the walls. K rations, opened and unopened, lay strewn about. The place looked like a pigpen. Infantry packs had been opened, the contents thrown about. This was the work of the Germans who had captured the men in the outpost, a hasty looting.

We cleaned the place up, then set about checking the abandoned weapons to see if they were still serviceable. Parts were missing from the machine gun and tommy guns. We finished destroying the machine gun, as it was beyond field repair. Then Angelly and I cannibalized the two Thompons and came up with one good one. The rest of the men did the same with the rifles. Soon we had several M1s that were also serviceable. Everything else we destroyed, throwing the parts outside and scattering them about.

That evening, after dark to avoid detection by the enemy, another squad relieved us after an exchange of challenge and passwords. We returned the way we had come, in squad combat formation with a scout out front, all eyes and ears alert to any foreign movement or sound. We entered town past the sentries, after challenge and passwords, and made our way to the large house where the rest of the platoon was staying. Here we turned in our newly acquired surplus weapons for redistribution. The next few days were spent in R and R, cleaning weapons and exploring a little outside. We scarcely mingled with the infantry, never telling them we were the 101st Airborne. We felt that should some of them be captured by the Germans in another enemy raid, what they didn't know, they couldn't tell.

We browsed about town, taking turns on outposts and small patrol duties. Everything remained quiet during our stay. The big offensive, Operation Nordwind, ordered by Hitler to isolate and destroy the Allied armies one at a time, did not fully materialize. The attack did jump off the night of 1–2 January 1945, with the enemy successfully crossing the Moder River between Haguenau and

Kaltenhausen and between Neubourg and Schweighausen, to cause havoc among inexperienced American companies of the 42d "Rainbow" Division and later capture the one raw platoon at Wickersheim. After recovering from the initial shock of battle, the green 42d Division rallied, counterattacked, and drove the Krauts back across the Moder River.

The 42d Division had survived their baptism of fire, minor as it was, counterattacked on their own, and now were on their way to becoming a fine reliable combat division that would hold their own through the end of the war.

Farther south, or upstream from us, the Germans still held one large "bulge" on our side of the river around the city of Colmar. This soon became known as the "Colmar Pocket." From this pocket the Germans constantly ran patrols into Allied land and staged shootouts with Allies who entered into or strayed near their domain. The Krauts here were becoming a pain in the Allies' butt. General Devers had decided to take care of this situation about the time the 101st was scheduled to arrive in his area. He intended to form a static line on the south shore of the Moder River from his farthest left flank all the way to the Rhine River on his right flank.

Lieutenant General Devers ordered the task force of his Seventh Army, along with the French First Army, under command of Gen. J. de Lattre de Tassigny, to attack, 25 January 1945. By 26 January, the day of our arrival in Alsace, it was all over. The Germans holding the pocket had all been killed, captured, or driven back across the Rhine River. The last significant German thrust of the war, Operation Nordwind, was ended.

On 31 January we received orders to move to Pfaffendoffen, a small town on the Moder River, just across from Niedermodern. We assembled as usual with full combat equipment and marched by foot in combat formation toward our objective.

After a mile or two with no sounds of war and no signs of battle-strewn wreckage or bodies along the way, we became a little more relaxed. Men would walk close to a buddy a short distance, talking, then move back to combat position. Others joked or talked to one another while we walked. We ate from our rations and drank, either from water canteens or bottles of schnapps or cognac.

Chmeliewski carried two large bottles of cognac in pockets he had improvised, sewn in each end of a long woolen muffler wrapped about his neck. As we walked, he would drink first from one bottle, then the other, each time hefting them, regarding them thoughtfully to see which was the heavier. Then he would drink again, feigning an attempt to bring both bottles to the same exact weight.

Near the end of our march Chmeliewski was in the friendliest of moods, laughing and joking with the rest of us as he walked on feet that seemed to find every obstacle on the road.

The march had been at an easy pace and we entered the small village by midmorning. We could see evidence of garden patches in and around the town, but nothing was growing at this time of the year. A decaying snow lay half crusty, half mushy on the ground that still held frost. The road dead-ended just beyond the last house on the left. Beyond lay scrub-brush fields, and beyond the fields, growing close to the river, was a large evergreen forest.

An enemy antiaircraft gun stood in the yard of the very end house. It was a 40mm, platform type, still intact and operational. Evidently the crew had simply walked or run away from it when things got hot, abandoning it without sabotaging it in any way. This was highly unusual. All military that we knew always rendered any weapons, vehicles, or equipment useless if they had to be abandoned. The enemy troops who had held this area prior to our arrival must have been the bottom of the line in quality.

The gun's pointing or aiming was controlled by small turning-wheels that would lower and elevate the barrel and swivel the whole thing around, like a carousel. This is exactly what we used it for, a carousel. With Borchers sitting on the bicycle-style seat and the rest of us sitting on the barrel and carriage, we passed Chmeliewski's bottles around, spun the handles one way and the other, and for better than an hour played as though we were kids again. It was exhilarating, with this sudden release of pressure, to see my battle-hardened comrades caught up in the same whorls of escape as I was.

Two husky farm girls and their mother had been busy with their chores, feeding the several cows in the barn and doing family wash with a scrub board and a tub set on a small brick firepot built just inside the main door of the barn. Now they stopped and stood staring at us in apparent disbelief.

How could we Americans fight and win a war when we were gamboling about like children and drinking cognac as though it were water? We did not take the war and its problems seriously enough. After watching us a few minutes they went back to their chores, shaking their heads and muttering to themselves.

The stay at the house was short. Before noon we re-formed and moved out across the fields and through the woods to take up positions at the far edge of the trees. From here we could command a broad view of the open ground down to the river and of the town and woods on the far bank. Every once in a while we would see an enemy or two moving about in the town or in the fields behind it. The distance was at a maximum for rifle fire, and our orders were simply to hold these positions anyway, so we didn't become interested or concerned.

We knew the Germans had observed our arrival but evidently they, like us, were willing to leave things just as they were and enjoy what little peace a man can get in combat.

We set about digging foxholes. This was the practice, always to start digging as soon as we stopped. A man could never tell how long he might be in one spot or if the enemy would attack or lay down artillery or if the Luftwaffe would show up, bombing and strafing. Any kind of hole, complete or just started, is better than the open ground. I can recall one stop-and-go march in which we covered only a few miles in which each of us must have dug at least a dozen complete foxholes. Dig or die.

Carl Angelly and I worked together. The digging was easy in the sandy soil, so we decided to make the hole large enough to be comfortable while we were at it. We had nothing else to do anyway, and digging helped occupy our time.

As we walked back toward the farmhouses, Carl recalled a number of large target frames the Germans had set up at the edge of a field. We pulled the wood target frames down and dragged them back to our positions. We used these to build retaining walls. Our hole measured close to eight feet by eight feet and was almost six feet deep. We braced our wood sidewalls, covered the top with heavy timbers, piled the excavated dirt back on top, and dug a zigzag stair-way entrance to our new home.

The doorway we covered over with an old piece of canvas we had found, placed straw at one end for our bed, and hung Carl's little oil lamp from the top center beam. This, we agreed, must be the most elaborate foxhole in all Europe. All the while we were digging and elaborating on our dugout, our platoon leader watched, smiling, and didn't bother digging a hole for himself. As darkness began to settle, he told us to be prepared to move out. We weren't going to stay here this night, and all our hard work had been for nothing.

As it turned out, however, we received orders by runner to stay in place and hold this area in a defensive position until further orders. The night grew colder and darker; the lieutenant came and asked if he could share our hole. "No, sir! There's just enough room for us," we replied—Liddle and Benson had moved in with us. Our platoon leader left to dig his own hole in the dark. So the little feud which began in the last days of Bastogne continued between the lieutenant and me. This may have been a mistake on my part, for with rank on his side he had more ammunition than I did.

Our stay lengthened to several days, during which time our over-sized "foxhole" became sort of a community room. We had space, a light, and a covered doorway. Troopers just getting off watch on the machine guns came to our hole to brew K-ration coffee on the squad stove and warm up. The men could brew coffee and smoke cigarettes without having to hide in the bottom of an open foxhole cupping the cigarette in their hands or under cover of a raincoat. Other men constantly came in to change clothes, socks, and take a helmet bath, or write a V-mail letter home. All night and most of the day we had company, but after a while we became used to it and managed to get our needed sleep.

Our second day in this position our platoon leader pointed to a spot on his map and ordered Carl Angelly, Liddle, Benson, and me to wait till nightfall, then move forward to the riverfront and set up a listening post in an old abandoned foxhole. Again I argued with the lieutenant that the foxhole was located on a slope at the edge of the river facing the enemy without cover or concealment. If a shoot-out occurred, we would not be able to fire in our own defense or make our way across the exposed open ground back to our own lines. We would all be killed.

"The purpose of this," the lieutenant explained with authority, "is to maintain a listening post so the enemy will not surprise us in a sneak attack. The men out there will have a machine gun hidden in the hole with them. If the Jerries attack, this forward post will give us warning and the few minutes necessary to prepare ourselves for the attack." Then, with a very dramatic look on his face, he added, "Those men out there"—meaning whoever was in the hole at the time—"will be just a handful of heroes."

We all looked at each other. This joker had seen too many movies. He was a new officer in our outfit, a replacement who had come to us shortly before we left Bastogne. His actual combat experience was limited, as was his time in the paratroops. After this incident the men began referring to him as "Yo-Yo."

Our officers, with the exception of Yo-Yo, were all good men. There wasn't a thing any of us wouldn't do for them or they for us. Most of our officers performed acts of daring beyond the call of duty in almost every engagement. They were leaders, not pushers, and they worked hard to prove this point, from first training, the runs, the jumps, and in combat. Until now we had been able to rely on our officers in wisdom, common sense, and combat leadership.

Sergeant Vetland argued with the lieutenant against sending anyone out there. He pointed out the logical reasons for not committing men and a valuable automatic weapon to such a vulnerable, ineffective, and irretrievable position, but the lieutenant would have it no other way.

We moved back to our "mansion" and sat about on the ground, cleaning the machine gun and other weapons and getting equipment ready that we would need for a twenty-four-hour stay in no-man's-land.

Shots rang out. Alfred G. Corgan, one of our new replacements, had suddenly noticed the Germans across the river and had opened fire on them.

"There's Krauts over there," he shouted. "Krauts, Krauts, shoot them, kill them." And he was banging away with a carbine at a distance that would be a long shot for a rifle.

A few shots from the enemy side and bullets chipped bark and thudded into trees around us. Troopers began returning fire as they hit the ground and went for their foxholes. The enemy fire increased, then ours increased. Bullets spattered through the trees, machine guns joined in, and a small war was developing.

"Now you've done it. I oughta kick your ass," Sergeant Vetland yelled over his shoulder at the rookie. "I hope they don't start throwing artillery."

He gave the command to cease fire. No matter what happened, no one was to fire again unless he gave the order. With our shooting stopped the Germans slowly ceased their firing, too, and soon all was quiet again. No one on our side was hit.

Vetland took the new man aside and for a quarter of an hour talked to him like a father. The man eventually became a first-class soldier but was killed later, fighting in Germany.

Long after it became totally dark, five of us shouldered our machine gun and tripod, plus two cans of machine-gun ammo each, along with our personal weapons, and made our way out of the woods. At the last minute the lieutenant had assigned a new man to our detail so we could break him in. We crossed a road, crept, bent over low, through barren farm fields past the shell of an abandoned farmhouse, and made our way silently down to the river's edge to the spot we had been shown on a map.

We found the foxhole, which was fully exposed on a slope of the riverbank facing the German-infested woods on the opposite side. Because of the exposed position of the hole we had to move into it quietly under the cover of darkness, stay there all day without allowing our helmets to show above the edge, and be relieved by another watch the following night. It would be crowded with five men in one hole during those long hours, and we couldn't enlarge the hole by digging; the enemy would see the fresh dirt, know we were there, and spend the rest of the day trying to drop a mortar shell on us.

It was here in Alsace that the army employed a new technique that had been developed during our fighting in Holland. Far behind our lines, usually behind a group of buildings, a battery of searchlights had been set up. The angle of their projected beams was such that they bounced off the heavier moisture or low cloud layers in the air and formed an artificial moonlight to glow brightly on the enemy's side of the river, to be turned on or off at our convenience. Our side of the river remained in total darkness.

Daylight came; it was a beautiful day for this time of the year. Although a light crust of old snow remained on the ground, the air was warm, the sun shone brightly, and there was very little wind. But here we were, stuck in the bottom of a damp miniature cramped dungeon. Time dragged. How could five men, sitting with their backs to the wall, feet to the center, over and under each other's, be comfortable for minutes, let alone hours, in a cramped wet hole in the ground? I read the looks on my comrades' faces. Their thoughts were the same as mine. Later, as our bones and muscles became cramped and aching, these thoughts became audible. It would be a miracle if that lieutenant lived through the war.

We munched K rations during the day, drank water from our canteens, and buried our refuse and excrement deep in the dirt beneath our feet. By midafternoon we were so many lumps of clay, not moving, for each movement circulated air between our soaked bodies, sending chills to the marrow of our bones.

Our minds were far away, thinking of such things as home, Paris, incidents of childhood, first love, huge steaks smothered with mushrooms, heavy wine, and firesides, all the thoughts that soldiers think.

Then the new trooper, without thinking, reached up out of the hole and threw his empty K-ration box and tins away. Immediately an alert German machine gunner fired long bursts at our hole, the striking bullets kicking dirt over us. Their mortar men watched the strike of his tracers, to know exactly where his target was. Within the minute a mortar shell burst behind us. We were shocked back to reality and hunkered low, forgetting for the moment our miseries.

The enemy now knew we were here and would keep trying with mortars until they finally got one directly on us. We would be turned to hamburger. We could not leave the hole—the run across the open field back to the vacant cottage was too far; the machine guns would cut us down long before we covered half the distance. We couldn't even stick our heads up, let alone put our machine gun up into firing position. We had to cower here and hope they were bad mortar men.

Then a welcome sound reached our ears, the *plong—plong—plong* of our 60mm mortar returning fire on the German mortar. We could hear our 60 firing even though enemy shells rained around us. Thomas was trying to zero in on the enemy gun by listening to its firing, judging the direction and distance, then firing two or three rounds of his own.

He must have thought he had it figured pretty close, for suddenly we heard the sounds *plong, plong, plong, clank, plong* . . . he had dropped the rounds so rapidly into the muzzle that as he was putting one shell in, he struck another coming out of the tube. We could hear the deflected shell turning over and over in the air, making a strange yodeling sound coming toward us. Thomas had been firing over our heads toward the Germans; now this round was going to fall short . . . and it would be close.

Thomas's wayward shell struck the very rim of our hole and exploded. So far he had come closer to scoring a bull's-eye than had the enemy. We joked, wondering just whose side he was on, theirs or ours. But Thomas must also have scored pretty close to the Krauts' gun, for the enemy mortar turned its efforts toward Thomas's gun. It became a mortar duel. A dozen more shells were exchanged; the enemy gun went silent. I don't know if Thomas had scored a direct hit or whether the Krauts had changed position or had just quit the contest. All the same, we kept very low in our hole, and very still, for a long time.

Well after the sun went down it at last became dark enough for our replacements, if there were any, to make their way to us. We expected a runner to arrive telling us to come in, that there would be no replacements. We could not believe that the lieutenant would actually send more men into that position and situation following the mortar duel. Nevertheless, he did, and after the whispered challenge and password, we crawled stiffly from the hole and watched as the other men slid reluctantly down into place. Then we whispered a few encouraging things to them like, "Don't worry, their mortar men can't hit a thing. Unless they bring up a new crew of expert gunners."

"If they start getting close with the mortar shells you can make it back to the woods if you run fast, low, and real zigzaggy."

Our replacements told us to drag our asses out of there.

We headed wet and aching back to our underground "mansion," which indeed appeared to be a mansion after our twenty-four-hour stay in a small hole partially filled with water. It didn't take long to get the squad stove in operation, and soon we were relaxed with a hot cup of K-ration instant coffee and a cigarette while our clothes hung from the top rafters to dry. We rubbed our hands and feet to massage life and warmth back into them.

I began to wonder if the lieutenant was in fact in a vendetta with me, or if he really just didn't know any better. If it were a personal thing between me and him, and now Carl Angelly, why would he have sent another patrol into such a ridiculous situation? Why would he have needlessly and deliberately endangered the lives of men, unless he just didn't know any better?

# 4 Patrol

The night of 31 January 1945, A and B companies of the 501st Parachute Regiment, with E company of the 327th Glider Regiment, attacked across the Moder River. Their orders were to shoot up the enemy's headquarters and troops and bring back prisoners for interrogation. In realty this attack near Neubourg was to pin German troops down in place while Corps made a bigger attack elsewhere against a larger foe on the American side of the river.

This raid went well, taking as prisoners of war one German officer and fifteen enlisted men, and leaving an estimated fifty enemy killed. Our casualties were one killed, one missing, and thirteen wounded. This one patrol took more prisoners in one night than the entire Seventh Army took or captured during the whole time that the 101st Airborne was attached to it.

On 1 February 1945 we received our first pay since before our trip to Bastogne. There was very little need for money in this area, so most of the troopers turned their pay back in for the purchase of war bonds. Some of the men bought money orders and sent money home. I was able to send three hundred dollars home to Mother, and like most of the other troopers I already had war bonds coming out of my pay regularly.

The big enemy Nordwind push that had been feared by VI Corps in this sector was not about to materialize. It had fizzled out after Hitler called most of his better fighting men back to the Fatherland to make a stand there, leaving most of the lesser troops along the Moder River and west of the Rhine to stall the Allies and fend for themselves. Our time was spent in patrolling to, and in behind, the Germans' lines.

The night of 3 February 1945 the 506th sent a platoon-sized patrol across the swollen Moder River. Two-man inflatable boats were brought up and hidden in the houses facing the river. That night, after the moon had gone from sight, the troopers carried the boats down the riverbank and silently slid them into the water. The current was swift and the boats hard to handle, especially for men who hadn't had the opportunity to practice with them. They fought the current as best they could in the small swirling boats, trying to keep them headed toward a target spot on the other side while the current did its best to sweep them away downstream.

The enemy had been on alert ever since our raid on 31 January. They thought we were planning a big push at this point. Why else the buildup in troops and extensive patrols?

They were ready. Mortars in the distance coughed, flares arched high, ignited, then hung suspended by small chutes above the river. The men were caught helpless amidstream in the sharp black-and-white, unreal contrasts of a pen-and-ink setting. The river's black mirrored surface reflected the cold brilliance of the flares, silhouetting the patrol in their own stark world of frozen hell.

German machine guns were quick to respond. Again the mortars sounded in the distance, this time belching out high-explosive shells instead of flares.

The men had remained frozen when the first flares ignited in the air, hoping they wouldn't be seen, but when the machine-gun and rifle fire lanced into them from the enemy side they had to paddle for their lives. The enemy fire was so heavy and concentrated that the patrol was forced to withdraw back toward the friendly side. A couple of the troopers' bodies were found downstream two days later.

An early thaw was setting in. The rivers were swollen far beyond their banks. Big gun emplacements filled with water; the dirt sides caved in, crumbling the sandbag walls into the holes. Our foxholes filled with water, many of them to within six inches of the top. It became impossible to stay in them and yet most uncomfortable to stay in the open, where the wind and air were cold and damp. The ground was saturated. Our boots remained soaked, as well as our clothes. The February wind cut into us. We existed the best we could.

On 5 February 1945 we received orders to move to the extreme right flank of the divisional lines and set up positions in Haguenau. We marched in combat formation on a route that generally paralleled the Moder River. As we entered Haguenau, I noticed a large picturesque house with many front windows, at the corner where the main road made a sharp right turn. We moved down the street lined on either side by tall narrow houses and buildings. There were very few buildings with walkways between them. Most were built tight together and so close to the road that no room was left for grass, just a narrow sidewalk between the front wall and the road. This was like walking down a deep man-made narrow trench. Troops caught in an ambush here would be in for a bloody time.

An order was given to halt. We fell out on either side of the street, some men standing, some sitting, everyone a little on edge, weapons at ready. We still didn't trust the civilians hereabout. Stories of civilian Nazis hiding on rooftops and rolling Teller mines down on troops below kept the men looking upward, keeping an eye on the roof edges for any sign of ambush. A movement, a shadow, anything—but if it did happen, where would one take cover?

A rattling sounded from ahead and above, near the rooftops of the tall buildings. Troopers instinctively tried to fade into doorways and small protected spots in the walls. We looked for Teller mines or grenades to roll down the slate roof and fall to the cobblestones and explode among us. Nothing happened, but someone was up there.

Several troopers kicked their way into houses. Some of them headed to the upper floors while others ran through the buildings to the backyards and alleys. It was too late. They caught only glimpses of very young and very fast kids flitting through small openings in the walls and fences, to disappear as though they had never existed. We'd lucked out—there were no Teller mines or grenades to fall on us, that time.

We re-formed on order and moved out. Those kids couldn't have been more than eight or nine years old and here they were, playing the deadly game of real war. Forced to choose between having one of our own killed or maimed by such tactics and having a civilian Nazi, regardless of age, die, I think any one of us would have killed the Nazi.

Company A took over houses and moved inside where we would spend the next several days. Second squad was assigned to a house nearly indistinguishable from the others that it was jammed in between, but it was comfortable and roomy enough. From Holland, Bastogne, and now here, we were at last out of the water-filled foxholes and the cold, biting wind. Just across the river, in the houses facing us, was the enemy. Yet, for the next few days, we went about our business as though we were a thousand miles from any action or enemy at all.

While here each one of us was issued two cans of American beer. It was warm, but it was American. Latrine rumors began, just as they always did in such cases. We heard from one or another that some religious people back in the States didn't want us to have beer, for many of our men, like myself, were under legal age for beer or whiskey. We grumbled about the rumors, true or not, took our two cans each, and sipped them very, very slowly, to make this nectar of the gods last as long as possible.

Most of our time was spent in weapons cleaning and inspections, close-order drill, physical exercises, and a few combat problems. It was more like garrison life, but not without the little spice of having the enemy just across the river whom we harassed a little now and then. From time to time we would sneak into the upstairs of other houses to fire a burst or two of machine-gun or rifle fire, or a rifle grenade, at random into windows over the river. At times we would set up a mortar in a hidden yard and fire several rounds, just to keep them on their toes.

Here the army set up portable showers that could handle a couple of hundred men an hour. This was a favorite pastime. If we had nothing to do or were not on some sort of detail, we would take two or three showers a day. What a difference from Holland, where we hadn't had a real bath for seventy-two days. We also began receiving mail, most of it several weeks old. Packages contained chocolate that had turned white and fudge that was hard as marble, but Mother always saw that I received fresh peaches picked before they had ripened, which she coated with wax and packed well with paper. They were usually just right when I received them. Mother also sent a good supply of sardines, crackers, and white divinity candy filled with black walnuts. All of which was shared with my squad.

I returned to my billet one day after duty to find my buddies sitting around eating a lot of goodies. "You just got a package from home," Carl said. "We saved you some."

Sure enough, a package had come for me and my squad had opened it for the treats my mother was famous for packing. On my bed I found two cans of sardines, some crackers, one peach, and several pieces of divinity candy. At least they had saved me some of the best of the food. All the men were grinning at me—they were proud that they had actually saved me something.

Again I found myself as squad leader of the 2d Squad and had just returned with several other troopers from the showers to our billet. I went to my sleeping area to bag my towels and dirty clothing for the laundry. Here, we were even having laundry taken out, done properly, and returned. We hadn't had it this good even back in England. And definitely not this good in Mourmelon-le-Grand, France. This was supposed to be front-line duty. Maybe this is the way the infantry fought and we just didn't know it.

When we received mail we'd normally sort through it to open the one with the earliest postmark first. It was here I opened a letter from my father. It was short, written in the heavy, scrawled hand I knew so well.

The letter started out: "Dear Bob"—my family name—"I have some bad news. . . ." It went on to tell how my brother, Elmer, who had joined the troopers before me, had had his left leg blown off above the knee. He had been struck by a mortar shell while fighting with the 511th Parachute Infantry Regiment on Leyte in the Pacific.

I was so stunned that I read and reread the letter, each time hoping the words would change, or just go away. They didn't. I walked slowly back to the house that my squad was billeted in, sat on the floor, and read the rest of my mail. The remaining letters prattled on about meaningless things, in a style calculated to boost the morale of a soldier overseas.

I couldn't believe it. Maybe it was a mistake. Memories of Elmer came to mind. We had been kids in the thirties, wearing corduroy knickers with long checkered argyle stockings, the dress for boys in those years. The days we had hunted together, Elmer striding through fields on long muscular legs. Our days in high school, running the miles there and back home to save our bus fare. The many days I had watched him running easily along ahead of the group, practicing for the high-school cross-country team. We were always running or walking, even in the paratroops. We were in Camp Mackall together and had run the same red sand roads; but now it was all over for him.

Other troopers in the room were reading their mail. At times one of them would read aloud to the others, just certain passages that were not personal and that the others would get a kick out of, like one big family.

The men of my squad saw my feelings and asked if something was wrong. I told them what had happened and they left me alone for a while, saying nothing. They knew full well there was nothing to say from one combat man to another, for we had all seen the results of arms and legs torn from bodies and there was no way in the world any of them could gloss it over for me.

A couple of days later, following the news of the loss of my brother's leg, I went with several of my buddies to the showers and movies that had been set up in the rear lines, to try and forget for a while. We spent the whole afternoon there, returning just before evening chow.

As we approached our billet, Luke Easly met us in front of A Company CP and informed me I had been volunteered to take a patrol across the river. I didn't believe Easly and went to the company command post to see what I had volunteered for. Sergeant Vetland told me that it was a patrol across the river but that no one had been volunteered. The command was asking if anyone would volunteer. So far no one had. I replied that I had come this far in the troopers, I might as well go the rest of the way.

"Sure, I'll take it," I said. Company commander First Lieutenant Kennedy sent me immediately by jeep back to G-2, where intelligence briefed me on what they wanted. One of the main roads passing through Haguenau crossed over a small bridge that was still intact. It disappeared among the enemy-held buildings on the other side of the river after first passing alongside a wide barren stretch of ground that ran from the river's edge to the first line of buildings.

The houses and buildings on the other side of the river formed sort of a semicircle around this flat, clear field and were believed to hold a well-armed enemy, backed by heavy weapons and artillery. It would be my job to scout this area, locate any heavy weapons that might be there, and get this information back.

We were not to expose ourselves or to take prisoners or unnecessary chances; G-2 wanted only the information on this trip. I would be able to take weapons and men of my choosing. I could also take as many men as I felt necessary to complete the mission. We would be backed up from this side by .30- and .50-caliber machine guns, 60- and 81mm mortars, 75mm howitzers, and 105mm Long Toms. I was issued a Very pistol, two flares, and a bag of grenades.

If the patrol got into a spot from which it could not recover, I would fire a red three-star cluster flare into the air, and all these weapons mentioned before would cut loose on prearranged targets at one time. This should send the enemy to the bottoms of their holes and basements and allow us running time back to the river.

As a final thought they cautioned me that the last three patrols had all met with bad times. One, described earlier, had been caught amidstream and been butchered. The other two had left their rubber boats on the riverbank, and though camouflaged, the boats were discovered by roaming German patrols. The enemy waited hidden nearby until the patrols returned and ambushed them. None of the second patrol made it back across the river. The third patrol, after being ambushed, had several men make it back but were shot up pretty bad.

This last patrol had taken several German prisoners, one of them badly shot up, but they had dragged him back to the river's edge anyway with the others. Then all hell had broken loose in ambush, the German was shot several times more, and the patrol had to abandoned him in order to make it back themselves. The rest of that night, the next day, and the following night that squad had to stay at their post near the river, listening to the badly wounded German gasping and gurgling through bullet-pierced lungs as his body lived on, refusing to die.

Two men crawled out in the dark to the river's edge and threw grenades in an attempt to kill the wounded enemy. They were tired of listening to his wheezing and coughing. One man was stopped from trying to swim the river to kill the German with a knife. Into the second day and into the night the men of the patrol had to listen to the wheezing and gurgling. It was getting on their nerves. Finally, during the darkest part of the second night, another trooper crept to the water's edge and, throwing grenades, managed to kill the German.

Returning to my billet I informed the men what the deal was and asked for volunteers to go with me. The men looked first at me, then at each other, no one speaking up. I went out and asked around the company, but the men were too content with the easy life that was ours at the moment and none of them were too eager to get themselves killed or crippled so near to the war's end.

Finally Carl Angelly said, "Oh, hell, if you can't get anyone to go with you, I'll do it." Then Justo Correa said that he'd go too. A young trooper from Intelligence also volunteered, a former German paratrooper.

The young ex-German soldier had spent time in the German army and had actually gone into combat with them but didn't agree with the Nazi Party. He and his close buddy deserted, made their way to England, and from there to the States, where they joined the American airborne. They proceeded to take parachute training at Fort Benning, Georgia, and joined the 101st Airborne Division in the intelligence section.

Both of these men went on patrol after patrol behind the German lines with almost every platoon, company, battalion, and regiment in the division. They felt they could learn more for our side than could the average American trooper and could possibly talk the patrol's way out of a tight spot if it happened into one. They were fearless and many times over proved their worth and loyalty to their newfound country and comrades. I shuddered to think what would happen to them if they should ever be captured and found out. Their reward for their service? Full American citizenship after the war.

All our buddies wished us well and loaned us things they thought we might need during the patrol. Vetland loaned me his tommy gun and luminous-dialed watch, cautioning me to keep the leather cover over the face so it wouldn't be seen by an enemy. Other squad leaders loaned the same thing to Justo and Carl and offered us grenades, but we had at least a half-dozen grenades each given to us by G-2.

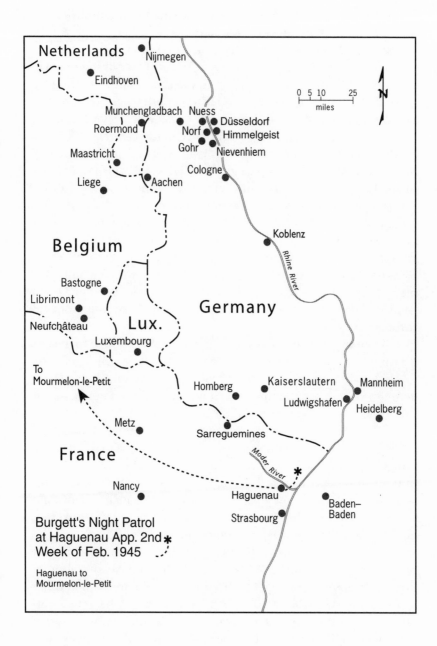

Burgett's Night Patrol
at Haguenau App. 2nd ✱
Week of Feb. 1945

Haguenau to
Mourmelon-le-Petit

We stripped off naked to make sure we had no identification of any kind other than our dog tags on ourselves that would give away our outfit's identification. We then redressed in ODs that had been searched with all pockets turned inside out and everything removed from them. We dressed in ODs, for they were soft wool and wouldn't make slight noises when scraped on brush or branches. We wore wool knit caps, no helmets, and blackened our faces and hands with soot from inside the large wood-burning stove in the kitchen.

All this while the other men kept kidding us about what the Germans would do to us if they caught us. "They don't keep paratroop prisoners, you know, they kill them. They'll make you run naked across a field and shoot at you with pistols."

"Yeah, but only after they make you talk, and when they work you over, you'll talk."

"Why don't you leave that shiny .45 pistol here, Burgett?" someone asked (the nickel-plated model 1911 .45 my father had given me). "It would be a shame to lose that to some lousy Kraut. It's so shiny that it will reflect and give you away. Some Kraut will shoot you through the guts for it."

"To hell with you guys," I said. "If they get close enough to see that it's shiny, it's going to be just too damned late for them."

All the while we had been taking the friendly ribbing, we had been getting ready. Justo disappeared suddenly into the bathroom and came back with a straight razor, tucking it in his belt.

"What the hell are you going to do with that thing?" I asked.

"Man, you don't know how close we're going to get to them Krauts tonight," he replied.

It was time. As we passed through the door, each trooper in the platoon shook our hand and seriously wished us luck. Then someone said, "We'll probably all be asleep when you guys get back, so don't make any noise when you come in."

A jeep from G-2 took us through the dark streets on a winding course to some tall houses on the edge of the river near the bridge. Reports from meteorology had been correct: the moon had disappeared from sight after 1:00 A.M. and it was totally dark. The jump-off time for this patrol was set for just after the moon was predicted to go out of sight. We were reminded not to forget the challenge and password for this night and the coming day, "GRAND—PIANO." I've never forgotten them since.

We had gathered behind tall buildings at the river's edge. Our German companion was there waiting for us. He told me that he had been on three patrols earlier that week. I mentioned to him that he didn't have to go this time but we would appreciate it if he did. It was time.

We had only one small two-man rubber boat, all others having been shot up in previous patrols and abandoned. Among the four of us we carried it across the road and down the steep bank. There we tied a long rope to the back and the other end to a tree, with most of the rope lying in a coil on the ground. We slid the boat quietly into the dark river, and the young German and I climbed in and started out. We dipped our paddles carefully into the water and pulled back with just enough force to keep from making the water gurgle. Carl paid out the rope between his fingers as we made our way.

We were limited to the power we could exert on the paddles to keep from making noise, and therefore the current carried us farther downstream than we had figured on. The damned thing was hard to control and wanted to swirl around end for end. It was only through concentrated effort and handling that we managed to keep it straight and headed generally in the right direction. All the while we were laboring and bobbing around I kept thinking of the other patrols, especially the one that had been caught midstream in the flares and shot to pieces.

We touched shore, which came as a mild surprise, for it was so dark that we could barely make out our landfall and all but impossible to gauge the distance. We landed just below the corner of a high wooden fence built in a large square. We climbed out. The G-2 man crept cautiously to the top edge of the riverbank, settling flat, eyes barely peering over the edge. I slid the boat back into the water and tugged on the rope three times to signal Carl and Justo to pull it back by the long rope we had attached to it.

Then I climbed up and in front of the G-2 man to keep watch while he slid back down to the water's edge to see how our two comrades were doing. They were in the middle of the river going round and round in circles, neither one of them ever having handled a canoe or small rubber boat before. Had we thought, we would have coiled another long rope in the boat, tied to the front, so we would have been able to pull them across without all the hassle. Finally they managed to make it to our side, swirling about end for end all the way.

Even without starlight or moonlight the sky remained a shade or two lighter than the dark ground stretched out before us. I had been lying flat as possible, clutching the tommy gun in my right hand, chin pressed against the dew-soaked grass, watching for any movement that might present itself against the lighter skyline. The night was too quiet. Any sounds we might make, even whispering, would be magnified. We would have to be careful.

The enemy wasn't firing at all, either, a sign that they, too, had patrols out. What if we ran headlong into one of their patrols? All these thoughts had been going through my brain while I lay there watching—the problems we might run into and what to do in each case.

Carl and Justo had lifted the boat carefully and quietly out of the water, placed the paddles in the bottom of it, picked up their machine guns, and joined me at the sharp ridge where the flat ground broke off at the eroded riverbank. My thoughts had been so filled with what might be ahead of us and in figuring exactly what to do or what our next move should be that I was barely aware of the boat being brought ashore and partially up the bank. I hadn't made a move to correct the act.

Now the immediate thought came to me, and I motioned for the rest to remain where they were while I slipped back down to the river edge. Taking hold of the bow and lifting, I slid the black rubber two-man craft back into the water and gave it a good shove so it would clear the edge of the river. It would be carried by the current downstream the full length of the rope, then swing back to the American side downstream from where the other end of the rope was still tied.

When I returned to the others waiting, Carl whispered and asked why I had gotten rid of the boat. "How the hell are we going to get back?"

"Swim," I whispered. "We're not coming back this way."

My plan was not to leave it onshore where it might be found by a roving patrol of Germans who would lie in ambush for our return, as had happened to the patrols before us.

Perhaps I should have made elaborate plans and briefed the others thoroughly on them, but there had been such short notice and preparation of equipment that I really didn't have a plan. Ideas such as pushing the boat back into the water and swimming back at a different point of return came as the G-2 man and I were struggling to paddle across the river. I recalled the other patrols and their ambush and the idea of ridding ourselves of the boat and how to do it came to me then.

We didn't know anything about this side of the river, so the best-laid plans would probably be worthless if we ran up against unforeseen problems. I felt the best way was to take it one step at a time and figure each move as we went.

Slowly I made my way toward the corner of the high fence. Justo and Carl followed while the G-2 man lay watching with his tommy gun at the ready. Arriving at the fence, I reached up, took hold of the top edge, and slowly and quietly hoisted myself up. Easing my head over the top, I strained my eyes. Large stacks of lumber filled the entire area. It was a lumberyard. I had never before seen a lumberyard in Europe.

Directly below me I could make out two chairs and a box with a military field phone resting on it. A listening post had been operating here. I wondered if the men operating this listening post had heard us and left the area. If they had, we could expect the Germans to put out patrols to intercept us, perhaps throw up flares, and certainly they would all be on the lookout for us.

I slid back down the wall and, with Justo and Carl, returned to the G-2 man, who was still watching the area ahead of us. Taking the lead, we started out and had gone no more than half a dozen steps when the sound of a mortar made its hollow metallic cough in the distance to our right front. We all hit the ground and stayed still, frozen in one position, not daring to move, breathe, or even look up.

I was lying with one side of my face pressed to the ground. Rolling my eyes upward toward the strange whistling sound, I saw and heard a flare suddenly spark, then sputter and burst into a brilliant white light. The stark difference between the searing white light and jet-black shadows gave the whole scene an unreal appearance of an unholy black-and-white celluloid negative from a photo camera.

This was another world, a place where nothing was real but the grotesque, flickering of extreme black and whites which danced weaving to a sputtering, sizzling sound coming from a gleaming white demon swaying suspended in the air below a trace of white smoke that plumed above. We lay still, not daring to breathe. Had the enemy seen us and even now were aiming their machine guns at us? I could almost feel the slamming of bullets thudding into my body, hear the fast ripping stitch of the machine guns hammering on us. The light flickered and went out. After watching that light I could see nothing. My eyes would not focus to the sudden darkness right away. I could not lead my patrol if I could not see. We would wait until our eyes adjusted to the darkness, then move on toward the enemy-held houses.

Another mortar coughed in the distance, this time a little farther to our right. We hit the ground again and closed our eyes, keeping our faces mashed against the wet grass. It seemed hours, but finally the sizzling noises stopped. The flare had gone out and again we started off, this time standing erect to make better time; we had wasted enough of it.

A shallow, narrow ditch ran on an angle from near the lumberyard toward a point where the bridge road entered the enemy-held houses. The Germans were great for digging small communication trenches to and from gun positions and forward posts to make it easier to man and maintain these positions even while under fire. I knew in my own mind that this was one of those trenches. I considered following it, but quickly dropped the idea. It was too conspicuous. The Germans were sure to have it mined, covered with some sort of alarm system, and also with mortars and machine guns. We took a course that led straight across the empty field, with no cover or concealment.

Thoughts of mines kept running through my mind, and with every step I expected to hear the beginning of an explosion. What I feared most was what we called a "castrator mine" (*Schu* mine). These German mines were about the size and shape of an ink pen and contained an explosive and a bulletlike projectile. Anyone stepping on one would have the bullet fired up through the bottom of his foot into the leg, and at the same time the concussion would blast upward, possibly destroying his manhood.

I had often heard of these mines and talked to men who had seen them and others who had been injured by them; but I did not recall actually having seen one myself at that time. I suspect they may have been used where I had been; I had just never had the misfortune of stepping on one.

Several more flares were fired, but we managed to follow the same procedure and hit the ground when we heard the mortar fire. We lay motionless, covering our eyes until the light died out, then stood erect and went on.

We finally reached the first building. It had a hole cut through the wall near the ground. The hole was about two feet high and about a foot and a half wide, a perfect machine-gun emplacement. Just as I started to look inside, there came the metallic rattling of a machine-gun belt of ammo being handled. I heard the box open, the cartridges rattle, and the bolt of the gun draw back, then close. The crew was checking everything to make sure all was in readiness. Evidently the Germans had been alerted to an American patrol in their area—perhaps by those who had been on the listening post.

Withdrawing from there and skirting around to the left, we made our way to another building. We crept close and could hear movements inside. There were enemy troops, but how many I could not say.

The four of us lay close together and by hand signs discussed the possibilities of throwing grenades into the house and capturing one or more of the enemy who would be wounded or stunned in the ensuing blasts. But after mulling it over in my mind, I figured that our main objective was not prisoners, but rather the location of gun emplacements and their approximate firepower.

Other mortars fired, sending more flares into the air to illuminate the area between the houses and the river. We were no longer in the open as before but had melted into and between the houses and were in no real danger from the flares. No two flares were in the air at the same time but were shot aloft in such a manner that one flare was igniting as the preceding one was burning out. At least the Ger-

mans had a good system of communication between their gun emplacements and troops at this point, to be able to govern their flare
firing to such a fine degree.

I counted each flare individually and the approximate position
of the gun as we lay next to the stone walls of the houses, the Germans on one side and we on the other.

We located a machine gun in another house, then another. Finally
we crept very slowly, very quietly, in single file back around to our
right and a group of houses that seemed to be set a little farther back
from the open field than the rest. Here we saw dim outlines of artillery emplacements, at least three guns. Whether they were the
dreaded 88s or 75s I can't say, but most of the Germans' guns were
the 88s. The flares became more and more frequent. Evidently the
Germans weren't sure whether or not we had continued on our patrol mission after our encounter with their listening post or had scurried back across the river to the safety of our own lines.

This didn't say much for the enemy's troops, not to send a patrol
of their own out to find out which we had done. They all seemed too
content to stay in their positions firing flares and straining their eyes
for us. Well-seasoned troops would have been out there hunting us
like beagles after a rabbit. Then again, maybe they did have patrols
out looking for us and we just hadn't run into each other yet. But
this didn't seem logical with all the flares being used.

We were nearing the lumberyard where we had first landed. This
I didn't like, and maybe the Krauts were waiting in quiet ambush for
us there, the way they had the other patrols. I stopped, let my buddies catch up with me, and then headed back more or less toward
the enemy but on a long circuit to our left, skirting the edge of the
enemy-held houses, keeping the houses to our right.

About three-quarters of the way around I led the way on an angle
toward the bridge over the river. We could see the straight line
against the skyline that marked the road. Finally we reached the water's edge about a hundred yards upstream from the bridge. We gathered together, gazing at the ink-black, swirling water. Even with the
enemy at our backs and safety just yards away in our own lines, we
were hesitant to ease ourselves into the swift, icy current.

How deep was it? How swift was it? How cold was it? Could a man successfully swim it? Men on other patrols had drowned here. If we did attempt to swim and got to the center, would our men on the other side start shooting before challenging? Would a German patrol come along, as we were helpless and struggling for our lives? Maybe they were watching us right now, just waiting until we did get to the center and couldn't return fire before they opened up on us.

"Well," I said, "this is it," and lay down on my side at the cold water's edge, opening my shirt letting the grenades I had carried there roll quietly into the water. I pulled the Very pistol and flares from my belt and slid them into the water also. The others did the same with their grenades to lighten the load for swimming the swift river. It would be hard enough to carry the fourteen-pound tommy gun and ammo.

For a few fleeting moments I had thoughts of firing a flare skyward and letting all of our backup firepower devastate the enemy positions, just for the hell of it. But one does not know what the ramifications of such an act would be.

"I'll go first," Carl Angelly said. "Cover me until I get to the other side, then I'll cover you."

He stepped silently into the chilling water and started out. He kept going but was walking, not swimming. Justo and the German-American G-2 trooper followed. I had been watching our rear and flanks and now went last just as Angelly reached the other bank. We were able to wade all the way across, the water just reaching our armpits. At each step we slid our feet slowly forward, feeling the bottom. It was a hard-packed soil bottom void of rocks, but the water was so swift that we had to be very careful not to lose footing and be swept away downstream, possibly to deeper water or into view of the enemy.

My men were all across and lay shivering, hugging the muddy bank. Carl had crawled to the crest, looking for friendly troops. I was still in water up to my armpits and several yards from shore. Each step had to be slow and careful, feeling along the bottom, fighting against the current. The river was mirror-black and freezing cold. My tommy gun was held high to keep it out of the water. I had waded many rivers and streams back in Michigan and was surprised not to find any rocks here. The river bottom at this point was clean and clear.

"Grand." The challenge word was whispered from one of the dark windows directly in front of us, but none of us could tell which one. The whispered challenge sounded like a thunderclap. Chills shot through me, for I knew a machine gun and probably a dozen rifles were pointing straight at us. Out in the water I didn't stand a chance.

I whispered the password, "Piano". No answer.

"Piano," I whispered louder, with a dry, croaking voice.

A short wait. Then, "Come on," a voice said. "Come on in."

My men waited for me to reach shore and helped me up. We climbed the embankment, crossed the narrow blacktop road, and scooted between the dark, foreboding buildings. Rocks and rubble lay piled and strewn between the houses. We stumbled and felt our way to a doorway and entered. Troopers asked if we were the patrol that had been across the river, the one they had been alerted to keep watch for.

"Yes." I answered. "Call G-2 and tell them we're back and to send someone to pick us up."

One of the troopers nodded and turned to the radio. Suddenly I began to shake violently. I don't know whether the chill of the river had taken hold or if it was a release of nerves. Probably a good dose of both. I looked at my buddies. They were shaking worse than I was.

Two jeeps finally arrived. Justo Correa, Carl Angelly, and the G-2 man were hustled into the first jeep and started off. I was put into the second jeep and we headed back to Intelligence Headquarters.

"Where in hell are you taking me?" I asked. "Ain't I going back with my buddies?"

"No, you've got a report to make. They're waiting for you back at G-2."

We sped along without lights through the dark night. Our jeep wound and jounced along narrow roads, amid piles of rubble and partially destroyed buildings. I sat huddled and shivering next to the driver. I was shaking so bad that I didn't care where we were going. All I wanted to do was get there.

At long last we pulled in next to a large multi-story, blacked-out building, got out of the jeep, and entered. The rooms were filled with officers, bright lights, maps on the walls, and desks piled with papers.

"Sit down," an officer ordered, pointing to a high, bar-type stool.

He held a cup of hot black coffee in his hand and sipped it as he walked about the room gathering small maps, pencils, and papers. He started asking questions as though he had been rehearsing them all night, sometimes asking the same questions over but worded a little differently. I felt as though I were being given the old "third degree." Suddenly he stopped, looked at me, and said, "You're all wet and shaking. How the hell did you get wet?"

I told him how we had waded the river and that I was half frozen. He looked at me for a moment, apologized, and stepped into the next room. Returning, he handed me a cup of scalding black coffee and a blanket to wrap myself in.

"Hell," he said, "I didn't notice. You must be half frozen at that. I thought you had a boat to come back in."

Then his attitude changed and he interrogated me as though I were a prisoner. I knew that all he wanted was vital information, down to the last minute detail, things that I might have forgotten, and this type of questioning would bring it out—things I might not have thought important enough to mention. He questioned me thoroughly, cross-examining until every word, every incident, checked and rechecked. During this time he had me point out the locations of the machine guns and artillery we had located on one of his smaller maps. He was good at his job, a master, and even while I listened to his questions and answered him, I secretly admired him, his method, his poise and coolness. He did a very thorough job of picking my brain.

He became very interested in the exact number of flares that were fired into the air while we were on the other side of the river, and he did ask me how many were fired. I answered a precise number without hesitation. This, I thought, was a way of his verifying the accuracy of my report; for G-2 had been able to count the amount of flares from this side while we were gone. He wanted to check and see if we came up with the same number. If we did, he could figure the rest of my report would also be accurate. I don't know why I had started keeping count and track of the flares fired but I had, from the first to the last.

He also seemed pleased when I told how we had returned the rubber boat and that it was still in our possession and could be used

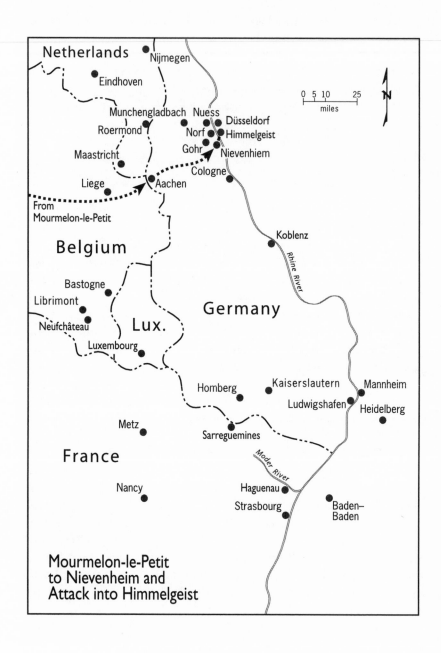

Netherlands
Nijmegen
Eindhoven
Munchengladbach　Nuess
Roermond　　　　Norf　　Düsseldorf
　　　　　　　　　　　　Himmelgeist
Maastricht　　　　Gohr　Nievenhiem
Liege　　　Aachen　Cologne
From
Mourmelon-le-Petit

Belgium

Koblenz

Bastogne
Librimont
Neufchâteau　Lux.
Luxembourg

Germany

Rhine River

Homberg　Kaiserslautern　Mannheim
　　　　　　Ludwigshafen　Heidelberg
Metz
France　　Sarreguemines

Nancy　　Haguenau
　　　　Strasbourg　Baden–Baden

Moder River

0 5 10　　25
miles

N

Mourmelon-le-Petit
to Nievenheim and
Attack into Himmelgeist

again on other patrols. When I recounted how we had managed to wade the river back to our side instead of swimming, he was surprised and highly pleased. This was excellent news. Up till now everyone had thought the river at this point was far too deep to wade and the only way to cross was by boat.

"That's great," he said. "Now you can turn in the Very pistol, the flares, and the grenades we loaned you."

"I haven't got them." I replied.

"What did you do with them?"

"When we started into that river we didn't know how deep it was. We only knew it was wide and cold, swift as hell, and that men had drowned there. We got rid of as much weight as possible so we wouldn't drown. We threw the grenades, the flares, and the flare gun into the river on the other side."

The G-2 officer flew into a minor rage. He lectured me on the high cost of each Very pistol, their scarcity, and their value. There were only two flare guns in the whole damned division and I had thrown one of them away. According to him I shouldn't have lost anything, not even a grenade, unless, of course, it was put to good purpose against the enemy. But to deliberately throw something away—never.

He paced the floor a little, gradually cooled down, and remarked that the fact that we had recrossed the river back to our side at a different point from our departure pleased him. He questioned me at length about the depth of the river, the height and angle of the bank, and the type of bottom on the river. Was it muddy, clay, sandy, would it be solid enough to hold a tank?

I answered the questions as accurately as I could and told him that in my opinion the river would not be a tank barrier if the banks could be cut down a little by a tank with a bulldozer blade going through first. Otherwise they might prove too steep and slippery for a heavy Sherman to climb. But I felt sure that, the water being only armpit deep and the bottom of hard-packed soil, a tank could traverse it easily.

He paced the floor, talking to himself and answering his own questions. "The river wouldn't be an obstacle to troops, either, then. They could wade across in great numbers at almost any given point. In other words, we could make an all-out assault and wouldn't have to worry about boats and all the other materials and problems that a waterborne landing would present.

"But on the other hand, we must think of the men. They must be in a good psychological frame of mind when they get to the other side. They must not be so wet, chilled, and uncomfortable that most of them would not be at their peak for combat."

Finally he called in other officers and they talked for what seemed to me to be hours. From time to time one of the other officers would ask me one or more questions and again they would consult maps and talk among themselves.

At long last they turned to me and said I should return to my unit. The jeep driver would take me back. I still had the blanket wrapped around me as we drove. The wind was cold and it was still dark. I didn't pay much attention to the route or dark silhouettes as our jeep ground and whined its way through narrow, rubble-filled streets.

At long last we pulled to a stop in front of the house in which my squad was billeted. I waved to the jeep driver as he pulled away, adjusted the ammo belt around my waist, slung the tommy gun on my shoulder, and entered. From the outside, the blacked-out building looked as though it were deserted, but when I entered, the whole 2d Platoon was sitting around the front room waiting. Vetland was standing near the stove and offered me hot coffee from a pot that sat on top of it. He grinned and asked me what had taken so long; all the others had been back long ago.

The others had been back long enough that they had changed to dry clothes, had a hot meal with hot coffee, and sat warming themselves by the woodstove. It was getting near daybreak and these jerks had sat up all night waiting for our return. I felt like a teenager who had tried to sneak in after hours and found his parents sitting up for him.

The next few days were spent in relatively quiet army routine, cleaning weapons, close-order drill, inspection, and so on. We moved out by truck 23 February 1945 to Saverne, where we stayed only two days, billeted in houses there. On the second day we marched down to the rail yards. Men were ordered to get baled straw from large stacks standing nearby and take it with them to assigned boxcars.

Sergeant Ted Vetland and Luke Easly carried a bale between them. The boxcars were small, much smaller than the ones we had been used to seeing in the States. The sides were marked *"40 Hommes—8 Bêtes"* (40 humans—8 cattle), but of course, in true military fashion, we were loaded well over forty men into each car. This was to be our first trip in the "forty-and-eights," which had gained so much fame in World War I, but not our last.

After being issued a day's supply of K rations, we loaded onto the train, spread the floor with straw, settled down to make ourselves as comfortable as possible, and made the trip to Mourmelon-le-Petit, not too far from our old camp, without incident. Day drove our tank back to Reims and turned it over to an armored unit there, then rejoined us on his own (after taking a couple of R and R days in Reims). Losing the tank was like losing a family pet, but it had been fun while it lasted.

En route the train would move so slowly at times that troopers would jump off and walk beside it for miles, just for the exercise. At other times, when the train picked up speed, some of the troopers would climb to the top of the forty-and-eights, where they could still walk up and down the length of the cars or just stretch out for more room.

Finally, after eighteen hours, we detrained in the center of a wide-open area near a large group of tents. Here we were formed into company and battalion groups and marched to where we were assigned tents that would be our new homes for who knew how long— a week, a month? Nonetheless, this was to be our new home until we would be needed again.

Our secondary barracks bags that had been stored in Mourmelon-le-Grand were brought by truck to the rail siding and dumped on the ground. Our officers allowed us to look through the great piles for our own and bring them back to our assigned tents.

These bags had also been looted by almost everyone who had handled them en route to us. Most of them were slit straight down the sides. And again everything, no matter how personal, how dear, had been taken. All that remained was a little dirty laundry.

I asked the company commander, First Lieutenant Kennedy, for permission to look for Speer's bag. He had bought his mother a hand-carved tortoiseshell comb while we were in Paris together just before Bastogne. We had pulled out of camp for that battle immediately on our return from Paris and he hadn't had time to mail it. I wanted to get it and send it on to his mother in New York. When I found his bag, there was nothing left in it, not even a pair of socks, just an empty bag slit down the side. How could rear-echelon non-combat troops, entrusted with our personal belongings while we were in combat, steal from us?

I looked long at the name "Siber Speer" stenciled on the side, and a feeling of disgust came to the pit of my stomach. I threw the bag to the ground and walked away.

# 5 Himmelgeist

Garrison life in the military returned to normal, even in Tent City. We started in with our regular morning runs, calisthenics, close-order drill, weapons and area inspections, and field problems. The only duties that were lessened were the wood-cutting details and the digging and maintenance of the latrines and other menial tasks. These were taken care of by the German troops we had captured in the battle for Bastogne.

A few days after our arrival in this camp we got up early in the morning, stripped to the waist as usual, and started out on a short six-mile run. It was snowing so hard that it was almost impossible to see the third or fourth man ahead. Our bodies turned red as beets and steamed as the snow melted on our bare skin.

Finally, on returning to our area, we came to a halt in front of the compound where German prisoners of war were huddled against their buildings to keep out of the biting wind and driving snow. They stood with hands in pockets, their large collars pulled high around their heads.

We came to attention on command, opened ranks, and began exercising under the commands and cadence counts of our noncoms and officers. My body felt as though it were on fire. My skin would feel the thousands of needlelike pricks as the wind drove the hard snow biting into us. I watched the snow accumulate on the head and hair of the man in front of me while the snow that landed on his body melted.

At long last we were brought back to attention and stood there staring straight ahead. Although our gaze was to the front, we could still see and watch the German prisoners of war behind their high barbed-wire fence. Some of them just stood huddled and glanced at us from time to time, almost timidly. Others would stand swinging their arms about rhythmically while shuffling their feet to keep the circulation and warmth in their bodies. Before we had been dismissed, nearly every one of them had stared at one of us at one time or another, then shook his head as though we were mad, or just a crazy illusion. No one in his right mind would deliberately stand out in the cold driving snow, stripped to the waist, and do physical exercise, just to impress an enemy that was already beaten and behind wires.

"Now we know why we didn't win in Belgium," one of them said aloud. "The *Amerikanische Fallschirmjäger* are all *verrückt,* crazy."

The time passed much in this same manner. Day after day our time was spent in what were now boring field problems, weapons inspections, goldbricking, and running a battle of wits between men and command—the command trying to think of ways to keep the men occupied and disciplined, the men trying to think of ways to get out of duty and find pleasant diversion, even to drinking themselves into a rosy, happy little world of their own.

It was here in Mourmelon-le-Petit that Carl Angelly, Hassel Wright, and I went AWOL (Absent Without Official Leave) for a night, slipping into town to see a movie and drink wine afterward. Later, feeling pretty good, we ended up just walking around town and came upon a small photo studio. We had our picture taken as a group, then each of us individually. (It is this photo of me at age nineteen that appears in several books.)

The towns in the surrounding area were small, the women were few enough for the multitudes of GIs, and restlessness and routine were our biggest foes. Our command kept throwing details and problems at us in an attempt to ward off the growing ferment. Our troops were well past due for a week of wide-open hell-raising and revelry. More and more tales of reckless abandon were circulating among the troopers. The top brass, I think, used this as a measuring stick to know when to throw the men back into combat. Let them vent their wrath and pent-up frustrations on a legal enemy.

We received news on 7 March 1945 that the Germans had failed to destroy the Ludendorff Railroad Bridge at Remagen and a patrol of the 9th Armored Division had fought their way across it to the other side to establish an all-important foothold on the German-held side of the Rhine.

Our training went on as usual. We trained and pulled field problems while the German POWs were kept busy doing the menial camp work. On 15 March 1945 we were ordered out, looking our best to pass in review for General Eisenhower and other notables, including our own commanding generals. The division fell out and marched a couple of miles to a large open field, where we formed up in divisional order of regiments, battalions, and so on. General Eisenhower then presented the 101st with another battle ribbon and a U.S. Presidential Unit Citation to the entire division. This was the first time in American history that a U.S. Presidential Unit Citation was awarded to an entire division. This award was in recognition for the division's stand in holding Bastogne during the Battle of the Bulge. Under command, we passed in review before divisional and other high-ranking officers, then off the field and back to Tent City of Mourmelon-le-Petit.

Again duties resumed as usual and our squads, platoons, and companies were fleshing out as our healed wounded began trickling back in from hospitals around the country. One of the men to return to A Company, along with others, was Donald B. Straith. He had come to us just before our trip to Bastogne with the "one-day wonders." Straith had been wounded in the hand our second day in Noville, 20 December 1944, and had shipped out that same day to a hospital far to the rear before Bastogne was fully encircled by the enemy. Now he, along with many others, was returning to the parent division.

Two days after we had received the U.S. Presidential Unit Citation, on 17 March 1945, the Ludendorff Bridge collapsed, leaving many American troops stranded. The whole operation was in peril of being aborted. This would mean another crossing operation, which might consume weeks and countless lives just to regain what was now in our very hands. But our troops held while a pontoon bridge was built and the war resumed, business as usual.

So it was, on 24 March 1945, that we were all stripped to the waist in the Company Street doing physical exercises after our regular morning run, when the sound of distant aircraft engines reached our ears. The noise became louder and louder. Then flight after flight of C-47s, C-46s, and twin-boomed flying boxcars began droning overhead, becoming an almost continuous bridgework of aircraft, heavily laden, lumbering and laboring their way toward Germany.

The entire formation from beginning to end, consisting of 1,696 troop carrier planes and 1,346 gliders, filled the sky end-to-end and side-to-side. Allied fighters riding shotgun totaled 2,153 fighter planes for a grand total of 5,195 Allied aircraft in one gigantic flight heading beyond the Rhine into Germany.

Our POWs behind wire looked skyward in dismay and awe, mouths open, faces frozen in bewilderment, staring with vacuous eyes. Never before had they seen such airpower as this flight of American planes, all heading toward their homeland, Germany. After a few minutes of their silence we could hear them murmuring over and over. *"Alles kaput, alles kaput, Deutschland ist kaput."* (Germany is done.)

Something big was happening. This was no practice or dry run; this was the real thing, a wet run. Paratroopers were heading for combat. We stopped to stare. Who was it? The 82d was as beat as we were. It wasn't a part of our division, the formation was too big. Was it the 17th Airborne? They'd had their combat baptism in Brest after Normandy and in the last stages of the Battle of the Bulge and were now fully experienced combat troops. Perhaps it was the 13th Airborne Division—they hadn't been baptized as yet. Whoever, it was not us; this time we got a break. The command was using someone else besides us.

As it turned out it was the 17th Airborne Division. The news, as we later received it, made this out to be the largest river crossing in history. This armada was made up in ground troops of the U.S. Ninth Army, the Canadian First Army, and the British Second Army. These ground troops crossed the Rhine at daybreak, some hours ahead of the airborne. The airborne included the U.S. 17th Airborne Division as part of the First Allied Airborne Army, and the British 6th Airborne Division. General Eisenhower, Supreme European Allied Commander, placed this whole operation under the command of Field Marshal Montgomery.

Montgomery's own 6th Airborne Division had been nearly wiped out under his command in Normandy when he left them in as line troops for weeks after their drop in Normandy, as he did with the 101st and the 82d in Holland—a gross violation of the cardinal rules in the use of airborne troops. We were surprised and elated to learn the British 6th Airborne Division was back in action, but more than a little dismayed that Monty would ever again be placed in command over any airborne or American troops. We should have known Monty was in command by the enormous size of the airborne flight: he would never make a move forward without having nearly the entire Allied command and their total supplies under his control. What was Ike thinking of?

All of our prior jumping had been from C-47s, and we were scheduled to make a practice jump from the double-doored flying boxcars that coming weekend to acquaint ourselves with the newest member of the airborne troop carriers. Now as I looked skyward I felt a relief; there would be no practice jumps for us now. I did feel compassion for those men up there, troopers and aircrews alike, making that trip into another D-Day, this time into Germany. We all knew something big was going on, and this time someone else was doing it. We also knew that a lot of men would die.

Later that day we watched the number of planes that returned. There were almost as many returning as had departed, a good sign. But this was war and there were still losses.

The 3d Armored Division, which had crossed the Rhine some days earlier upstream, began driving in a large pincer movement around the Ruhr Valley to begin the encirclement of well over one- third of a million Germans there. The American 2d Armored Division began a breakout drive on 1 April 1945 deep into German territory to swing clockwise around the north of the valley. The 3d Armored, coming up from the south, was to swing counterclockwise, and all were to meet up with one another at Lippstadt. This encirclement was to become known as the "Ruhr Pocket." The Germans held out stubbornly, for the Ruhr Valley was the center of the German Krupp arms manufacturing empire, the heart of the German military might. From here flowed the tanks, 88s, small and large arms, cannons, and all the tools of war. The Ruhr was the heart of Germany; cut the heart from the beast and the Nazi war machine dies.

It was the beginning of the end. The next day excitement ran high among the troops. On Friday, 30 March 1945, orders were received to get ready, we were going in again. We stitched scrap bits of cloth over our divisional shoulder patch or covered it with tape, this being the standard rule whenever we were in transit. The following night our advance party left for the Ruhr Pocket. The next day, Easter Sunday, we began drawing additional weapons, ammunition, knives, clothes, and all the necessaries for war and killing.

On 2 April 1945 the large open trailer trucks pulled into the area. We loaded on them in orderly fashion and again settled to the straw-covered floors and again moved out in a long, strung-out procession. All these actions were only too familiar; it was like listening to an echo and reecho, or looking into a mirror that reflects in multiple another mirror on the opposite wall. This was the same thing over and over again, to infinity.

More than sixteen million men were in the American military in World War II, and fewer than one million total of them did all the fighting in all theaters—a fifteen-to-one ratio of noncombatants to fighting men. The rest were in units that directly or indirectly serviced the combat men, the men on the line. This was the main reason we were in constant combat. With sixteen million men, there was no one to take our place.

We had received our orders. Preparations were made. We moved out; again we were committed. This time it would be to the end. It had to be.

Our division command had set up headquarters in Glehn, between München-Gladbach and Göhr, with Düsseldorf just across the Rhine River to the east. Our convoy had taken a route that led through battle-devastated Aachen. The city had been so ruined that not one building escaped destruction. A path had been cleared by American bulldozers through the brick and stone rubble piled in the streets to allow transportation to pass through. Bloated cadavers of cattle and horses were scattered everywhere. White towels and bed sheets were hung from existing window openings and wherever by civilians to signify their submission.

On our arrival the entire division, with the exception of the 501st, made bivouac in and around Glehn. The 501st remained in France, along with the untried 13th Airborne Division, was scheduled to make parachute jumps into prisoner-of-war camps ahead of our thrust to liberate Allied inmates, some of whom were of high political or diplomatic rank. But as it turned out, the crumbling fall of the Third Reich occurred before any of these units could participate in "Operation Jubilant." Here the 501st Regiment and the 13th Airborne Division sat out the final phase of the war, always on the edge of the chair.

Our division sector lay on the Rhine River, which at this point was so crooked that we were actually covering a front of about twenty-four miles. The 327 glider riders were to our left, with the Erft River separating their sector and ours.

We had detrucked in Göhr, where our regimental headquarters was stationed, and each battalion headed out for its own little sector. We were lucky: the 2d and 3d Battalions drew first duty on the lines while we, the 1st Battalion, relaxed in reserve. We walked in strung-out formation as we always did, entering a small town. Here we took over houses, but there were no civilians to argue with about who was right or who was wrong in taking them over. The civilians had all cut out.

There is always something foreboding about entering a town that is completely without a living soul. The civilians were always in such a position that they could observe the Germans withdrawing, how far they withdrew, how much fighting equipment they carried, and if they were seasoned troops or not. They would then observe the pursuers, evaluating them in the same manner. Here lay an almost reliable barometer of the near future, the immediate reactions of the civilian population. If there were no civvies in town on our arrival, or if they were leaving with their belongings as we entered, we were probably up against a seasoned and stubborn, dug-in foe. And the fact that we were also seasoned and stubborn meant that a lot of real estate was going to get torn up, along with anyone who got in between the enemy and us. If the civilians remained, we would have little or no fighting.

The company commander billeted my squad in a house near a corner intersection. It was a large house but had very little furniture in it. The former occupants must have taken it with them. As squad

leader I was called to a briefing in the company CP. When I returned
I found we had two new additions to our squad, a replacement by
the name of Bill Surface from Virginia, and Robert Hull from Ohio.
I asked Surface if he knew how to operate the machine gun. The men
of the squad laughed.

"What's so funny? I asked if he knew how to operate a machine
gun."

One of the men said that Surface was no rookie, he had spent
more time in the chow line than I had in the army.

"And how much combat time does he have?"

"Well, none, that's what he said."

"Then I don't give a damn if he was born in the army. Some men
spend their lives in the service and never fire a weapon of any kind.
I want to know if he can operate a machine gun. Surface, do you
know how to operate and maintain a machine gun?"

"Yes," Surface replied, "I can handle the weapon."

"Well, you're our new machine gunner now. Our last regular one,
Bielski, got killed in Bastogne. The rest of you guys, when I ask someone a question, keep your mouths shut and let that man do his own
answering."

As I turned and started busying myself with my gear, Surface settled to the floor next to the gun and began inspecting it, to famil-
iarize himself with it. I watched from the corner of my eye. He
seemed to know what he was doing. He took the gun apart and began cleaning it. The other man, Robert Hull from Toledo, Ohio, was
quiet and seemed to want to do whatever he was told to do. He became a rifleman in our 2d Squad.

On 5 April 1945 we moved to another town. We walked, as usual,
in combat formation, even though it was apparently safe enough
here. As we entered town, the company commander assigned each
squad to a certain house for billets. We entered ours. It was a large,
rambling two-story place with a large front room, or more like a
recreation room. A pool table stood in the center of the room, a
wood-burning stove near the center back wall.

We claimed sleeping spots, built a fire in the stove, then settled
in to sit and drink from bottles of schnapps and Cognac appropriated in our travels. And tell stories. Suddenly I remembered that to-

day, the fifth, was my birthday. I was now twenty years old. The squad all drank to that. Bottles were passed around more and more frequently, and as each man drank, other troopers would tell him how much of a kid he was, or a little old lady, he should be able to hold the bottle up longer than that. "Let's see some bubbles coming up." When the bubbles were coming up, the whiskey had to be going down.

A few hours later we again received word to move out. Picking up our seaborne rolls, we fell outside, shouldered our weapons, and headed out walking. As we walked the men talked and kidded each other as usual. One might tell of the good-looking, well-built girl he'd had, in this town or that. And how she was madly in love with him. Then several other troopers would almost always remember the same girl and the intimate times they had also had together.

This is the idle talk of soldiers as they walk countless miles over almost impassable roads, through the foot-clinging mud, the choking dust, and the rubble of torn-up towns, all the while bearing their packs, seaborne rolls, and weapons—the heavy machine guns, mortars, baseplates, and bazookas—plus all the ammo for these weapons. Sometimes, if it were available, we would also carry our food in the form of K rations. Putting the mind to work on something else and forgetting the body (it would function on its own, respond to orders, and do what it had to do), the miles slipped by, the loads lightened, and discomforts were forgotten. This is the way we traveled, mile after mile, day after day, month after month, through country after country.

We entered another small town, Nivenheim, and the platoon was assigned a house to stay in. It was a large three-story place with huge rooms filled with furniture. Sunlight streamed in through oversized curtainless windows that gave the place a warm, bright look. The blackout curtains had been pulled back and fastened to the wall. These blackouts would be put back in place before darkness fell.

Men scurried about, laying claim to beds and choicer sleeping spots. It was an unwritten law in the company that when a trooper or troopers laid claim to a spot or bed, he would lay his helmet on it and no other trooper would infringe on his claim. Most of the beds had two or three helmets on them.

Carl and I bypassed the first floor, raced upstairs, and were first to reach a good double bed in a large sunlit room on the second floor, to the very rear of the house. We put our helmets on it and went about the business of surveying our new surroundings. On our return we found two new replacements of another squad reclining on our bed, our helmets on the floor. It took some persuasion, almost coming to blows, to convince the new men that this was our property and to brief them on some of the unwritten laws.

Life was pretty quiet and comfortable the next day or two, as it had been for the last few weeks. We weren't in a life-and-death struggle of combat now but were being moved around in key positions or strategic spots. We griped and bitched about moving so much, but it was far better than the combat we had been through from Normandy on. All of us were now looking forward to the end of the war, when we could return home, alive and whole.

We were called out for company briefing on the morning of 11 April 1945. We were to make an attack across the Rhine River into the Ruhr Valley. Our purpose was to disrupt the enemy, check on the quality of their troops, and take a few prisoners.

The Ruhr Valley, with its huge stockpiles of raw materials, artillery pieces, tanks, ammunition, and factories, had to be taken.

The Germans, being what they are, refused to budge from the place that, both physically and morally, represented so much to them. Their main hope was to stall the Allies as long as possible in hopes that Hitler would come through, producing one of his promises of new and awesome weapons that would wipe the Allies from the face of the earth.

In our briefing we learned that we were to cross the river in company strength the night of 11–12 April 1945 and make an attack on the town of Himmelgeist, just below Düsseldorf. We were to capture that town, take prisoners, and hold positions there as though this were a major attack into the Ruhr Valley. When the Germans moved their armor and troops against us we were to fall back across the river.

Just after dark we assembled and marched to a small group of rubbled buildings close to the riverbank. The night was dark, damp, and cold. I felt a shiver rack through my body every once in a while but knew it was more from nerves than from the weather.

We were too used to living outside to let this weather bother us, especially after Bastogne and Haguenau.

Then we moved out of the buildings and down to the river's edge. A group of army engineers waited with small assault boats, each equipped with a gigantic fifty-horsepower outboard motor. All my life of rowing boats and paddling canoes on the lakes, rivers, and streams of Michigan, I dreamed of someday owning an outboard motor— not the size of these, but one that could get my boat around the lakes. My interest piqued; I talked with the engineers, asking many questions. They told me these motors stood six feet tall, weighed two hundred pounds, and were full fifty-horsepowered units. I couldn't fathom anything so awesome.

There was evidence of a pontoon bridge on the shore, but it had been almost totally destroyed. We had to make the crossing in small assault boats, somewhat like the ones we had used in Holland. But there the Canadian engineers were the ones operating them.

Going into Normandy, I had looked down into the dark waters of the English Channel. Crossing into Carantan, I had looked down into the dark waters of the Douve River. Helping troopers of the British 1st Red Devil Airborne Division back from Arnhem, I had looked down into the dark waters of the Rhine River. Crossing into German-held land across from Haguenau, I had looked down into the dark, swirling waters of the Moder River, and now, here I was gazing down into the dark, swirling waters of the Rhine River again. If I were to die, I hoped it wouldn't be in a cold, dark, lonely river. To have my body sink below the surface to bump along a muddy, slime-filled river bottom was a thought that agitated me.

Ridiculous as it may sound, these were my thoughts as we milled around, silently awaiting our turn to load, twelve men or more to a boat. Our footing slipped and slid around a little on the wet bank as we boarded, but we made it in good order. We lay flat along the bottom evenly on either side, heads toward the bow, feet toward the stern, to present less of a target to the enemy and also to stabilize the boat with a lower center of gravity. Then we would all be speeding, motors wide open, heedless of noise, toward the German homeland.

The last troopers to board took hold of the gunwales and heaved. The boats slid into the Rhine. Motors roared to life, the boats shot forward, and we were on our way; there is nothing noisier than a military fifty-horsepower outboard engine at full throttle on a very still night on the water. We went racing over a dark, foreboding river, toward an even darker shoreline. Spray showered over the sides onto us, not enough to drench us but just enough to let us know we weren't dreaming. This was real.

Without letting up on the throttles the engineers drove their boats full onto the opposite bank. There was the engineer's warning: "Hold tight, brace yourselves." Then, *scrunch,* and a grinding sound as we came to a jarring halt on the east shore.

We wasted no time. The men were almost crawling over each other in their scrambling efforts to get away from the water's edge. We were foot soldiers and preferred to do our fighting on good old terra firma. The water, no matter how little or how much, how shallow or deep, belonged to the navy.

We formed up in the dark without too many orders being given and started out. This was more like a mock maneuver than a combat mission. The whole company was scattered out in platoon and squad formations and moving full-scale down a fairly wide road toward Himmelgeist. This wasn't the leapfrogging, the door-to-door or hedge-to-hedge fighting, we had been used to. But our command wanted the enemy to feel that this was a full invasion of the Ruhr. Our moving out boldly and noisily would cause the enemy to move their troops against us, that we might test their quality and strength.

All became quiet except for the shuffling sound of troopers' boots, the creaking of body harnesses, and the occasional sounds of heavier crew-served weapons being shifted from shoulder to shoulder. I watched the silhouetted figures of the men moving ahead of me. For the most part all I could make out was the upper halves of their bodies against the lighter skyline. Then I felt someone reaching out, feeling my arm, then clutching hold of my sleeve. "Who is it and what the hell do you want?" I asked. A voice answered, "It's me. Robert Hull. Can I hold on to you while we walk?"

"Why?" I asked.

"Because," he whispered, "I'm night blind. I can't see anything at night." He then admitted that he couldn't hear very well at night either. Hull wanted to hang on to me and let me guide him through the night.

*Jeezus*, I thought. How in hell did a man like that get into a combat outfit, and why, in the first place, knowing his problems, had he volunteered to get into a combat outfit?

I took his hand and placed his fingers through the back center of my cartridge belt. "Hang on and don't lose me," I warned. Then an afterthought: "What the hell are you going to do if I get killed?"

"Get another guide," Hull responded without hesitation.

We were at the edge of town. Trees and brush hid the figures of the men ahead from being silhouetted. Those of us who were following behind kept contact by listening to the minute but familiar noises made by our comrades up ahead. They were feeling their way into enemy-held territory, going by instinct.

Suddenly shots rang out, tracers lanced back and forth, shouts and cries filled the air. We hurried forward. Some men were milling about, while voices that seemed to come from far away yelled not to come straight ahead. There was a tank trap, a deep one, right in the middle of the road.

I could barely discern the outline of a bunkerlike ramp in the road. Heading for it, I suddenly saw Surface's silhouette rising at the top of it; he was carrying the machine gun. Suddenly he disappeared from sight. John B. Woods, Earl Borchers, Justo Correa, Carl Angelly, several others, and I started up the slope as a small mob. I told Hull, "Hang on, don't lose your grip." "I won't," he replied, "I'm hanging onto you like glue."

Hull had good eyesight in daylight but when the sun went down, so did his sight. With Hull hanging on we reached the top of the obstacle and found it to be made of logs and packed dirt. On the other side was a deep pit, which had been formed when the dirt was dug for this improvised ramp. There were no mines set around it. At least we didn't discover any. We could just barely make out and hear figures of men grubbing around the bottom of the big hole. Some were looking and feeling for weapons, grenades, and other things they had lost when they tumbled bodily into the trap. Surface had located his machine gun and was climbing up the opposite side and out with it.

A tank moving down the road would have to go around this obstacle, which was almost impossible, for the stone walls and fences on either end formed another barrier. If the tank were to climb over, it would crash to the bottom, from which it would be impossible to get out.

Firing was getting heavier and heavier up ahead while we scrambled down into the pit and climbed up and out the other side. By the time my group got to where the firing was going on, it had all but stopped. It was only a token defense by very few old and very young civilians, nothing serious. One of the defenders had challenged our patrol with a "Halt" and got himself shot and killed for his patriotic blunder. A church steeple stood out against the lighter sky. Some one said, "It's an observation post, put a bazooka rocket in it."

A bazookaman moved forward and took up position behind a brush-covered stone wall. He knelt, took aim, and fired. *Fwoosh!* The rocket, streaming a fiery trail, launched forward in a brilliance of backflash from the bazooka. Up in a clear arch it went, right past the church steeple, then down to explode somewhere in town. A clean miss of the steeple. But in a far-off edge of town someone got a rude awakening.

Another rocket was loaded and fired. Another miss and another explosion in the outer reaches of Himmelgeist. Some troopers gathered around the poor gunner, giving advice and telling him how to do it. Some of the men even wanted to take turns on the bazooka. Others laughed and joked; this was almost like a picnic. A smattering of shots came from the center of town up ahead but nothing to get alarmed about.

Another man I thought was Charley Syer—it was difficult to tell in the blackness—moved into position and aimed his bazooka. "Let's go, let's go," the voices came from up front. "Let's hubba hubba one time." We had a job to do and couldn't hang around here all night practicing on an old church steeple.

"I'll get the son of a bitch," we heard the gunner say as we headed for the center of Himmelgeist. Another rocket scribed an arch in the dark sky, there was an explosion: the gunner had gotten the steeple. If there was an artillery observer up there, as there must have been, for all church steeples in Europe were used as observation posts, he was gone now. The steeple stood without noticeable damage, but it was done for the present as an observation post.

We made our way down the street. Several grenades were thrown into windows of houses suspected of having German soldiers in them. A few Germans in civilian clothes ran into the streets to surrender. We took them along as we made our way to the rendezvous spot where, on our signal, the engineers would pick us up with the assault boats. They had returned to the friendly side of the Rhine after dropping us off on this side.

My squad had the job of setting up a protective position to cover and hold the landing site of the boats on the riverbank. We set up the machine gun near the corner of a building close to the road running parallel to the river. Bill Surface, Carl Angelly, and a third man stayed with the gun. Surface, who had carried the gun all this way, allowed Angelly to take position as gunner while he rested a little. Luke Easly told the men on the machine gun to open fire if anyone came up from the left of the bridge. We would be going to the right to clear the river edge of possible enemy. Luke Easly, I with Hull hanging on to my belt, Smith, and several others moved down to a small wooden dock protruding a short way out into the river.

We made our way to the dock, clambered down to the right of it, then followed Luke in combing and searching the bank in that direction for two to three hundred yards; it was difficult to tell the exact distance. Retracing our steps, we passed under the dock, searching the riverbank at least two hundred yards in that direction. All was clear as far as we could determine. Again we returned to the dock. Here Luke, acting squad leader at this time said, "Follow me." Then, instead of going back under the dock, without thinking of his last instructions to our machine gunners, Luke made his way up the bank on the left side of the dock facing the water from the shore. We protested, but he repeated his order.

Following him up the bank, we stood for a moment, then started toward the position of our machine gun. A machine gun burst out in long strings of fiery bullets. They cracked between and around us. We all hit the deck. I slid over the edge of the bank from the side we had just emerged from, dragging Hull with me, and flattened against the wet ground. The rest of the men were around me, Hull still clinging to my belt. That wasn't a German machine gun, it was one of ours. In fact it was ours. Luke stuck his head over the bank and yelled. "If you can't shoot that goddamned gun, get someone who can."

*Oh, no,* I thought, *that was an open invitation for Carl to open up again.*

He did. Long bursts of machine-gun bullets plowed and raked the riverbank and wood dock, sending geysers of dirt and splinters of wood showering over our prostrate forms. We all yelled at once, "Carl, it's us, it's us, don't shoot, it's us." For a moment I thought of taking a shot back at him, just to get his attention.

"Stand up and show yourselves," Carl yelled.

We stood up, but I stood real close to the edge of the bank, ready to drop behind it if he started shooting again. After some yelling back and forth at each other we made our way cautiously to the gun crew. "What the hell's the matter with you?" Easly yelled at Carl.

Carl answered, "You said, 'If anyone comes up the left side of the dock, shoot.' I saw you guys go down the right side of the dock. Then a half hour later I saw shadows of a patrol coming up the left side and I thought you were Krauts and I fired. Then you yelled about my not being able to shoot right, so I fired again."

Carl Angelly was right, Luke Easly knew it, the matter was dropped, and we consolidated our positions of defense with the machine gun in our center. Luckily no one had been hit. At least we knew that Angelly could be depended on to fire when needed.

The rest of our platoon showed up some time later and dug in positions near our gun up on the road. It was our job to secure and protect this landing site for the company. I took several men of the 2d Squad and went to the river's edge to the right of the dock. When the rest of A Company arrived, it would be coming from our left, some on the road, some along the river. I liked having the dock pilings between me and anyone coming toward me through a dark night.

We waited. Time dragged; soon it would be daylight. Then we heard the shrieking of big shells coming in on us. The enemy had started his counterattack. Thank God—we had begun to think they were just going to ignore us and we would have to stay here another day or so.

The big shells landed, exploding violently around our positions as we hugged the ground. We could hear more shells striking the other side of town where we had first entered. Those of us who were down at the very edge of the water couldn't dig foxholes—they would fill with water at the first shovelful. Our radioman, Benson, yelled to us, "I just received word. The Krauts are bringing armor against us. When it gets here we can go home."

The shells continued coming in, most of them in our area. Small-arms, rifle, and machine-gun fire sounded from the center of town. The rest of A Company was working its way toward us. More shells landed on our positions with deadlier accuracy. Someone in town must be acting as observer—I thought we had gotten rid of him in the church steeple. The shells weren't hitting on us by mere guess-work or luck. We should have blown the whole damned church steeple away.

Finally word came down to get ready to move out. Our purpose in this attack had been accomplished: we had caused damage to German morale and to their city and tested their quality as soldiers and their strength. It was time to leave.

It had been our job as 2d Squad, 2d Platoon, to hold and protect this sector of river beach against all enemies for the purpose of a landing spot for our assault boats. We would also have to wait until every man was on board and ready to shove off for the friendly side before we could pull out of our positions and get in the boats.

We waited. After a time we could hear the movement of troops heading our way. Then we could make out glimpses of shadowy forms moving into our positions and melting into the ground. Three men of the engineers appeared to set up a tripod affair mounted with a long-barreled light with a pistol grip attached. One of the engineers aimed the light to the opposite shore, the signal was given, a flash of light returned the signal, and we could hear the assault boats start on the other side of the Rhine and head toward us. The long-barreled light kept aim while the operator flashed intermittent signals to keep the boats on track while they fought the river's current to our pickup spot.

We lay listening to the incoming shells. Their bright, fiery explosions turned everything around us to rubble. The smell of burnt powder was heavy in the damp air. Dust from the crumbled bricks and stone of the buildings and walls filled our lungs. A fire started, giving off an eerie orange glow that cast weird shadows around our end of town and reflected in bright sparkling facets on the river's choppy surface.

Time dragged. We could hear the sharp roar of the assault boats' outboard motors, but for a long while it seemed as though they came no closer, but buzzed like so many unseen giant bees in the distance.

Finally we saw them, vaguely at first in the glinting surface of the Rhine. The boats swerved, headed on an angle against the current, and beached where we waited. Figures materialized from the ground and headed for them. Men of A Company acted oblivious to the incoming shells and moved at their leisure to the boats, loading the wounded first, a few to each boat so there would be others not wounded to tend them.

We were the last to board the boats, for it was our job to hold the beach until the last moment. Just before we loaded, we ordered the German civilians we had retained as prisoners back to their homes. We had no use for or need of them. *"Raus, raus, gehen Sie,"* troopers ordered. The prisoners looked bewildered and hesitant at leaving. Again we ordered them to leave. They began walking toward town but kept stalling, looking at us. I think they thought we were going to shoot them down as they walked away. Then they were gone unharmed into the darkness. At a given signal of the engineer in charge we moved out in a swarm, a miniature armada, toward the friendly side.

Some of our men had been hit during the shelling, how many and how badly I didn't know. The medics had bound their wounds as best they could and made them ready for transport back in the boats. We also had four dead. Their bodies we had to leave behind for the time. They would be recovered in a day or two by one of our patrols.

The German artillery was accurate and followed us all the way back across the Rhine. I believe it was coming from German tanks that had arrived just as we shoved off. Artillery adjusted by observer would not have been able to follow speeding boats that accurately and keep constant contact with their shells. It had to be coming from tanks that had visual contact with us. The barrage rained around us with fiery explosions, sending among our small craft huge geysers of brightly illuminated water that soaked us all with spray. I became fascinated by the shells that landed close by. I could hear a shell coming in, watch the plume of spray as it struck, see the explosion as a brilliant green ball deep in the water just to one side of us, and then came the geyser rising high above our heads. Our boat was still intact as we struck the river bottom on our side of the Rhine.

We looked toward shore. It was still a long way off, or so it seemed. The trooper in the bow of the boat didn't want to get out, saying he didn't know how deep the water was. I yelled to him that it couldn't be that deep or we wouldn't have struck bottom. I stepped over the side, took hold of the gunwales, and started to pull, but the boat was too loaded and heavy for me to move alone. Several more troopers, seeing me standing in the water, got out to help, then all got out. The boat lightened and with everyone pulling we hauled it the rest of the way to shore. Here I was glad for the experience I'd had with boats and canoes. I knew from past experience that we were probably stuck on a bar that ran just off and parallel to shore.

Men of the company were gathering in the rubble of some nearby buildings, most of them shivering and soaked to the skin. I had been in one of the very last boats to leave, yet other boats were still coming in that had left before us, shells still falling around them. Perhaps their pilots had become somewhat confused with the darkness, the current, and the shelling. These things happen.

Suddenly there was a scream for help. Two boats had been turned over by close exploding shells. I heard Corgan call for help. He had been severely wounded and had been bound tight with bandages about the arms and chest in an attempt to stop heavy bleeding. In this condition and with the swift current he didn't stand a chance even if he were an expert swimmer. Two men, one of them Thaler, shed their clothes and dove in to swim in the dark searching for Corgan, but after what seemed a very long time they returned empty handed. Corgan and others had been caught in the swift current and drowned almost within reach of shore.

We lay soaked and shivering in the ruins of the buildings and houses until every member of A Company was either present or accounted for. We had eight men drowned and four killed in fighting and shelling. We formed up in combat formation and walked back to our billets. No one talked, no one boasted of our mission, no one laughed at the funny little things that had happened on the other side, we just walked.

Angelly and I went to our room, changed clothes, and climbed into bed to get what sleep we could. For long minutes I lay awake, feeling a little guilty—for two of the men who had lost their lives in the drowning were the two new replacements who had tried to take our bed. I thought for a little while that maybe I should have let them have the bed. But then again, we had been right, it was our bed and I had gone many more nights without sleep or even a good place to sleep than either of them had. I had been right but I couldn't help think of the lifeless body in a current bumping along the bottom of a muddy, slime-filled river.

As we lay resting, Carl turned on a small radio left behind by the former tenants; perhaps we could get Axis Sally and listen to her propaganda and some American music. A broadcast came on in a man's voice. The language was definitely not German. I couldn't understand it except for a name of a town or city now and then. Evidently someone was giving out plenty of propaganda against the Allies. Then we caught the name "Frranklin Delinski Rrozenfeldt." Carl and I burst out laughing. "Did you know that our president was a Jew?" Carl asked.

"No, but it sure as hell sounds like it," I answered.

Several times over we heard the name of our president mentioned, "Frranklin Delinski Rrozenfeldt." Someone must really be giving him hell for something.

Most men of the company slept well until midafternoon, when we were again ordered to fall out and be ready to move out on foot. We marched in combat order to another small German town named Norf. On entering the town we passed a command post. A trooper came from the building. Whether it was an officer or enlisted man, I don't recall, but he called out in a loud voice that our president Roosevelt was dead. He had died 12 April 1945.

I was stunned; we were all stunned. I looked about in disbelief. This wasn't possible, he was the only president I had ever known. He was the United States. But it was true. The radio broadcast Carl and

I had listened to in Nivenheim mentioned "Frranklin Delenski Rrozenfeldt" several times. Now we understood. President Roosevelt was dead and someone by the name of Harry Truman was now president. Who the hell was Harry Truman? None of us knew. I barely remembered my dad talking of Roosevelt and Hoover when that election occurred in the early thirties, but I'd been too young to understand.

In front of the regimental command post a large billboard-type sign had been posted out front with a large map of Europe displayed. Two white strings were pinned in such a way on the map that one string represented the Allies' lines on the western front, the other the Russian front. The strings could be moved and repinned to show the progress of the two fronts. At one point the two lines were coming very close together. Several German civilians stood examining the map, shaking their heads in disbelief.

Houses were commandeered from civilians, who were allowed to take bedding, a certain amount of clothing, and several minutes to get out. Again we were assigned billets. Again the same rush for the best sleeping spots and we were home, until ordered to march again. We felt no remorse in putting the civilians out for a few days, more or less. We felt they were all Nazis; they had started the war; they had destroyed countries, cities, and families; we were far from home; and many of our comrades were dead or crippled because of them.

A couple of days later a patrol of volunteers prepared to return in broad daylight to recover the bodies of our four slain comrades whom we had been compelled to leave on the other side. Jack Bram, squad leader, would lead the patrol of seven A Company men. They formed up at the river's edge without fanfare or notice to the company that they were going back. Jack Bram, without a helmet as usual, and his men slid their boat into the water, then all got in and began to paddle. Our engineers, with their assault boats and outboard motors, had left the area. Jack and his seven-man patrol had to paddle the distance in a wooden boat. They crossed the Rhine without opposition and no artillery firing on them.

After landing they met no one and were unopposed. They searched and discovered that German civilians had buried all four of our men in a common grave and placed a white cross to mark that they were Americans. The cross was inscribed: *"Hier ruhen 4 Amerik. Soldaten gef. 13 4 1945."* (Here rest 4 American soldiers, killed in action 13 April 1945.) Our attack had been the night of 11–12 April. The Germans, according to the date on the cross, must have buried our men early in the morning of 13 April 1945.

Jack Bram and patrol returned, bringing with them the bodies of Charley Syer, Alex Abercrombie, Marco Santillan, and Floyd Roberts, handing them over to our medics, who in turn would see that the Graves Registration Team would take proper care of them. Charley Syer had had his back almost torn away by a shell burst that also killed the other three troopers. Ten others were reported missing; it was later confirmed that six of those missing had drowned. Two days after that we recovered two more troopers who had drowned, their bodies washed ashore nearly two miles downstream from Himmelgeist. I never learned if the last two men were ever recovered.

As later reported, our night attack on Himmelgeist had caused the enemy to move their reserve troops and whatever armor they had in the area in a counterattack against us. By 13 April 1945 our armor in the east had broken through the Ruhr's defense and had made great inroads in the Ruhr Pocket. By the fourteenth the Pocket was completely cut in half. The end of the Ruhr Pocket could not be far off now, and we would no longer be needed here. It would be time again to move out to another strategic spot.

On the sixteenth the eastern half of the Pocket fell completely to Allied hands. On the seventeenth we were relieved by the 302d Regiment of the 94th Infantry Division. The fighting here over, what little there was of it, the 302d Regiment would have a fairly easy time during their stay in this sector.

On 18 April 1945 the entire German Ruhr Pocket collapsed. It was all over here. Untold amounts of enemy arms and ammunition came into the Allies' possession, along with 325,000 prisoners. We felt that we had contributed a little to the success of the Ruhr's collapse by our attack in Himmelgeist. In the last hours of fighting, the German command had issued mimeographed discharge papers to their troops with blanks left to fill in their names, making them civilians. Many of them put on civilian clothes or partial civilian dress, laid down their arms, and walked calmly out of the area, showing their discharge papers to the Allied soldiers who stopped them.

These reports quickly reached our command. General Maxwell
D. Taylor, commanding general of the 101st Airborne said, "Like
hell, they're still Nazi soldiers whatever clothes they wear or whatever piece of ersatz paper they carry. Take them all as prisoners of
war. If they think they can kill Americans until the last day, change
clothes, and say they are civilians when they have lost . . . No. They
are prisoners of war and will be treated as such."

Many of them protested, waving their discharge papers when
rounded up, but it did them no good. They went along with the other
prisoners still in uniform and were treated in the same manner.
Within the next two weeks it was reported that more than one million Nazi soldiers had been taken as prisoners of war in the Ruhr Valley and surrounding area. Here, it was over.

Company A, 506 Regiment, in a briefing while on a battle march in the Ruhr Valley. Sergeant Vetland, top center with back to the tree. Bill Rary, far right front. Don Burgett, far right behind Rary, facing left with back to the camera. (courtesy Mark Bando)

Troopers of 2d Platoon, A Company, take a break during a march and listen as one of its members plays a guitar. (courtesy Mark Bando)

Sergeant Jack Bram, front center without helmet, and his patrol ready to recross the Rhine into Himmelgeist to retrieve the bodies of our comrades killed there a couple of days before. Bill Surface upper left standing. (courtesy Mark Bando)

German civilians had buried our four slain comrades, Charley Syer, Alex Abercrombie, Marco Santillan, and Floyd Roberts, in a common grave. A member of the patrol shows deep feelings at the action of the enemy burying our dead. (courtesy Mark Bando)

Regimental Headquarters in Göhr. Troopers and German civilians check a large map on the progress of the Allies in the west and Russians in the east closing in toward Berlin. (courtesy Mark Bando)

After a train trip by forty-and-eights from the Ruhr Valley, Company A boards DUKWs "Ducks" in Ludwigshafen, Germany, heading toward Berchtesgaden. Dale Jacoby second from right, Don Burgett third from right, Sgt. Robert Impink fifth from right, Justo Correa sixth from right, Robert Hull, standing behind Justo and Impink. (courtesy Mark Bando)

Germans in full retreat hastily abandon war equipment along the highways. Note the worn tires on the towed artillery and other equipment. (courtesy Mark Bando)

Disillusioned, war weary, hungry, and beaten, German troops on the roadsides trying to surrender, then seeking instructions where to go when we couldn't accept them as POWs. We were on the move forward. (courtesy *Epic of the 101st Airborne*)

Later, on the autobahn, we encountered multi-hundreds of Germans all wanting to surrender. We were not in a position to take them as POWs and ordered them to start walking toward Munich, which they did. (courtesy *Epic of the 101st Airborne*)

Deeper into Germany on the autobahn we ran into full divisions of Germans, 12,000 to 14,000 men to a division, all begging to surrender. Bivouacs of POWs were formed in the open on the highways so the following U.S. military could feed them, give medical aid to those in need, and start the process to send them home. (courtesy *Currahee Scrapbook*)

We rolled down the Alps aboard "Ducks" into Landsberg and the horrors of concentration camps. The buildings on the right are German military barracks and warehouses filled with nearly every tool of war known to man. (author's collection)

A few bodies of the multi-hundreds of victims experimented on, tortured, starved, and murdered greeted our sight in the concentration camp at Landsberg, Germany. (courtesy *Epic of the 101st Airborne*)

Nuns, or nurses? Our medics sought out and brought these women into the camp to help the tortured victims and ease the last moments of the dying. (courtesy *Epic of the 101st Airborne*)

Jewish and Polish women along with other nationalities were used as "medical" guinea pigs by Nazi doctors. These women survived Landsberg's experiments, torture, abuse, and degradation. As happy as they were to be liberated, none could smile; many cried. (courtesy *Epic of the 101st Airborne*)

Landsberg's male guinea pigs, Jews, Polish, Czechs, Russians. All suffered years of "medical" experiments by Nazi "doctors" and torture by Nazi guards. They too cannot smile but stared us with vacant eyes. (courtesy *Epic of the 101st Airborne*)

Later we moved by semi-truck again, passing through devastated towns and cities. Wrecked trains on ruined tracks and buildings with empty windows can be seen in the background. Harold Phillips is third from the left, I am to the right of the pole leaning on the side of the trailer, Dale Jacoby is to my left, Carl Angelly is standing behind us, Walter Dobrich is standing in the front of the trailer grinning. Due to our diminished number the trailers are not crowded. (courtesy Mark Bando)

One of the many houses we requisitioned for our billets during our push across Germany, Bavaria, and Austria. Upper: John B. Woods, third from left, Carl D. Angelly, fourth from left in doorway, Floyd Smith, sixth from left, Robert Hull, far right. Lower: Earl Borchers, third from right, Hassel Wright, second from right, author, Donald Burgett, far right. Note the fur collar on author's coat mentioned in this book. (courtesy Mark Bando)

First Battalion, 506 Regiment, marches on foot into Hitler's resident city, Berchtesgaden, Germany. (courtesy Mark Bando)

Hitler's home, the Berghoff, bombed by the RAF just before our arrival. Within days it was thoroughly looted. Even stair treads were removed. Hitler's home, along with the nearby SS barracks, was ordered destroyed within weeks after our arrival and the debris buried secretly so that no monument to Hitler could ever be built of salvaged material. (courtesy *Epic of the 101st Airborne*)

Civilian newsmen and rear echelon officers brought in to examine Hitler's home. This view is the living room with a huge fireplace and large window overlooking a beautiful view of the Alps. Note the window (destroyed by the bombing) lowered down into the wall when it opened by electric motor. Also note the hot water radiators in front of the window that supplied heat for the house. (courtesy *Epic of the 101st Airborne*)

Hitler's retreat atop Kehlstein Mountain far above Berchtesgaden (now a public restaurant). This was not Hitler's home as it is mistakenly referred to at times; it was a retreat built by and from the German people as a birthday gift to Hitler. The Führer visited it only once on its presentation and never returned. (courtesy Mark Bando)

German officer surrenders to Maj. Gen. Maxwell D. Taylor in Austria. (courtesy Mark Bando)

Lieutenant General Theodor Tolsdorf, called "Tolsdorf the Mad" by his troops. Commander of LXXXII Corps surrendered his troops intact to Col. Robert "Bob" Sink, Regimental Commander, 506 Parachute Regiment. General Tolsdorf earned his nickname for his daring solo patrols behind Allied lines. He had been wounded eleven times. (courtesy *Currahee Scrapbook*)

Major General Maxwell D. Taylor had Hermann Goering's art collection, which had been looted from conquered countries, carefully moved to this building to be evaluated, catalogued, identified, and returned to its rightful owners. The men gathered around General Taylor are known art appraisers brought in for the monumental task. (courtesy Don Straith)

Bruck, Austria. First Lieutenant William C. Kennedy, the last Company Commander of A Company, stands before his orderly room. Kennedy received his captain's bars within weeks after this photo was taken. (courtesy Robert Hull)

Some troopers of 2d Squad, 2d Platoon, A Company, Lend, Austria. Rear: left to right, Carl D. Angelly, Earl Borchers, Donald Burgett, and John B. Woods. Front: left to right, William Surface, a liberated Czech, and Robert Beausejour. Note: All the pistols are pointed at the Czech. A combat man's joke. (Don Straith)

Bruck, Austria, 2d Squad. Rear: left to right, William Surface, Earl F. Borchers, John B. Woods, and Luke Easly. Front: left to right, Carl D. Angelly, and Joseph P. Nardi. (author's collection)

Taxenbach, Austria. Second Lieutenant Anthony C. Borrelli. Lieutenant Borrelli was usually the officer of the day whenever I was sergeant of the guard. He was an experienced combat officer, well liked by all who served with and under him. (courtesy Mark Bando)

Lend, Austria. Author, right, was Sergeant of the Guard as Harold Phillips, left, and Leroy S. Parsons (who took the photograph) made their way to Zell am Zee on pass. (author's collection)

Zell am Zee, Austria. Sherwood C. Trotter, fought from D-day Normandy, through Holland, Bastogne, and the balance of the war. One of the most fearless men I have ever known. Trotter was on pass in Zell am Zee when I saw him sitting on a bicycle rack near the boathouse and took his photo. (author's collection)

Joigny, France, long after World War II and our tour as army of occupation had ended. We were awaiting orders to return home and made one more voluntary parachute jump to maintain jump status and pay. Walter Dobrich, with unidentified trooper in background readies to board C-47. No equipment, a "parade ground jump." (courtesy Robert Hull)

Joigny, France. Author, Donald R. Burgett, right, and Bill (Creepy) Surface, left, stand in the shade of a Waco glider while waiting their turn to chute up and jump. Bill got the nickname "Creepy" due to his profession, an undertaker in his family-owned funeral homes in Roanoke, Virginia. (courtesy Robert Hull)

# 6 Merchingen

Early in the morning of 16 April, A Company formed up in the main street of Norf, the order to "move out" was given, and we began another march, this time to Weckhoven, south of the city of Neuss. Civilians were ordered from chosen houses. They were told what they could carry with them and the time frame (in minutes) in which to gather their belongings and leave. Our troops were usually in the houses helping the civilians to gather their belongings and speed them out the door. Again we consoled ourselves, "Better them than us." They'd started the war and we had spent too many nights out in the open in Holland, Bastogne, and in Alsace. At least the civilians had the homes of relatives and neighbors to go to.

The next couple of days we rested while our command received orders and made arrangements for our transportation. During this time many of us visited one of the many DP work camps that had been set up for laborers, mostly Polish men and women, who had been put to work in the many factories in the Ruhr Valley. In the camp the barracks were weatherproof. The compounds were of bare ground surrounded with high barbed-wire fencing. The inmates were of all nationalities, mostly Poles, with Russians, Czechs, Yugoslavs, French, Belgians, and anti-Nazi Germans. Most of these people were thin from not quite enough food but not like the starved skeleton figures we were to meet later.

These people were out of work with no source of food and no place to go. Survival instincts led many of them to follow us back to our billets, with most gravitating to our kitchens and food supplies. We had received orders that no DPs would be allowed to stay with any military unit. But we couldn't turn them away, and we put them to work in our mobile kitchens or handling menial tasks for which they were well fed. The ones who wished to stay with us we provided with old American uniforms to wear and hid them whenever officers came around.

One DP I recall was a young blond Polish girl of about fifteen or sixteen. She would have been very attractive if she weren't so damned skinny, but all DPs were skinny. She had a pleasant personality, always laughing and very bold, or naive. She sat with us, drank, talked, joked, and freely discussed sex as though one were talking about the weather. This was a novel experience for most of us younger men coming out of a simpler Depression world into the military. Though she expressed herself freely she didn't allow anyone, including her own people, to get familiar with her.

She told us how the Germans had invaded her village when she was very young. How they had taken her whole family, along with other families, on a freight train and had used them as slave labor. Her job was working with pick and shovel on road building and repair. The greater part of her life that she could remember was either behind barbed-wire enclosures or working on roads doing the work of a man. If any of the laborers didn't keep up with their work or produce to the satisfaction of the Germans, they were shipped out to camps with ovens.

I questioned her about doing a man's work with pick and shovel on the roads. How was she able to keep up? She replied that even though she was feminine in appearance, she was stronger than most men. We had been sitting around drinking a horrible, foul-smelling grog from a pot brewed up by the DPs that looked like brown sewer water that had been set on the wood stove to heat. It not only looked like sewer water but also had a taste that I imagined sewer water would have if one drank it. The girl told us it was made from potato peelings fermented to alcohol.

During this drinking social she laced her fingers together, left hand to right hand, and dared any one of us to pull her fingers apart. First Phillips tried unsuccessfully. Then another trooper tried with the same results, and finally I tried but could not break her grip. She only laughed at our attempts. Then she proposed that any two troopers could try. It was embarrassing, but two men did try, one man on each of her arms, pulling in opposite directions. They could not pull her hands apart.

I have never seen a man, even a hardworking one, with that much strength in his fingers.

A couple of years before, her father had been separated from her family and shipped out on a train packed with older Poles. Then, a few months before our arrival, her mother had been shipped away in a train loaded with older women who had all become too old and weak to work. Her mother begged not to be separated from her children but to no avail. Now only she and her sister were left.

I asked if she knew where her sister was now. She hesitated for long moments, looked at the other DPs gathered in the room, and finally pointed to an older girl across the room with dark hair and looking nothing at all like her. "That's her, that's my sister," she finally replied. The older girl moved to her side and put an arm around her saying. "Yes, we are sisters." After that the two girls stuck together like glue. Where you saw one, you would see the other. I doubt that they were truly sisters but now they had each other, now they were sisters; together they were a family.

These girls stayed with us, working in our kitchens and doing the men's laundry whenever we were billeted, then hiding with other DPs in baggage cars or trailers when we were on the move. They, with others, stayed with us all the way through Germany, Austria, and back to France. Months later, when they finally left us, the girls were no longer the skinny DPs they had been. They were filled out, their hair fixed, and with makeup and the flush of youth in their faces, some of the troopers stopped looking at them like adopting fathers or big brothers and a new look took its place.

In Austria they dated freely, joined our beer busts, and were treated with the respect the troopers would have shown a girl back home. I don't know what they might have been forced to do before their liberation, but the last time I saw them they were very independent and very American.

Many DPs stayed in camps that had been established for them until they could get their strength and some clothing and supplies. Then they headed off in the direction of their homeland, knowing that if any other member of their family or village were still alive, they would head for home also. It was just about the only way they would be able to find each other in a war-torn world. A half-starved people, adults and small children, started to walk across Europe to a home that to many was only a vague, shadowy memory—some of the younger ones not knowing who their parents were, or their true nationality. If they spoke Polish, they headed for Poland. If they spoke Czech, they headed for Czechoslovakia. The Jews headed for wherever their secondary language would take them. How many of them would make it?

The twentieth of April 1945 we again received orders to move out. We formed up in the main street and marched on foot to a rail yard in the vicinity of München-Gladbach, where we drew six K rations each and were assigned about fifty men each to forty-and-eight boxcars. The six K rations meant we would be on the train at least two days, possibly three. We were told to get bales of straw from a nearby stack, which we did, carrying the bales to our cars, Sergeant Vetland and Luke Easly carrying one between them. The boxcars were amply sprayed inside with DDT, the straw spread over the floor, and we loaded up in our assigned boxcars. Many of those loading the food and baggage cars wore ill-fitting American uniforms, some looking strangely feminine.

Men complained of the overcrowding. The "forty-and-eights," meant to hold forty people or eight cattle per car, were stacked with more than fifty troopers each. The complaints didn't last long. The weather was getting warmer, and being overcrowded was better than walking and carrying our heavy crew-served weapons and ammo. We didn't know where or how far we were going, but it would be at least two days' travel.

Our 101st Airborne Division was now attached to the American 7th Army in a wild pursuit of a fast-retreating German army. The enemy was retreating faster then we could follow, but this was their backyard and they knew all the shortcuts and they were blowing bridges and other obstacles up behind them as they went. But where could they go? With the Russians coming in from the east, the British from the north, and the Americans from the west and south, it was going to get crowded in the center sooner or later.

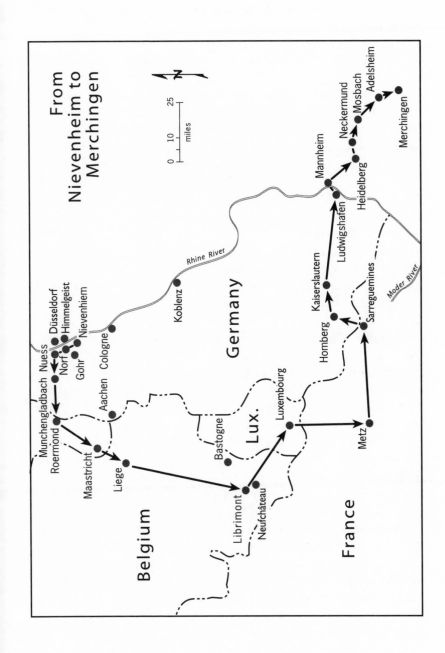

From
Nievenheim to
Merchingen

Our train finally started with a few uncertain jolts, slowed, and jolted again. I don't know if we had a paratrooper or an army engineer to operate the engine pulling our train. Whoever it was, I hoped he knew just when we were supposed to pull out and in what direction we should be headed. In the end we were rolling, slowly, but rolling. All the cars stayed hooked together. We were on our way.

The train moved as before, mostly traveling along pretty slowly, with troopers getting off at times to walk beside it. Then again it picked up speed and we were rolling along at a good pace, enough to cause a breeze to blow through the stuffy, well-packed car. When this happened we would all cheer as though it were a great event. Some men would climb to the tops of the cars to ride where they could be out in the fresh air, but they had to keep a lookout for low bridges. At times the train would slow and finally come to a full stop, sitting there for long periods of time.

Men took turns sitting or standing in the open door to watch the passing landscape and wave to people in rural areas, most of whom were preparing to fit their fields for the planting of new crops. Some of them waved back, some didn't—they just leaned on their farm tools, staring after us. Our only water was what we carried in our canteens, our only toilet facility the open door in the side of the car. From time to time a trooper had someone hold his belt while he leaned out as far as possible to pee in the breeze. There were no rest stops on this trip. If the train had speed and the wind was right, fine sprays would carry back into the door of the car behind us, creating a lot of yelling and cursing from those in the doorway of the following car. But they in turn took great delight in doing the same thing to the car behind them. And so on down the line.

Leaving Germany our trip took us through Roermond, which was in Holland, almost due west of München-Gladbach, Germany, down through Maastricht, Holland, Liège, Belgium, and past Bastogne, Belgium, to Libremont, France, and Luxembourg. At times our train would sit still for minutes or an hour or two before continuing on— even backing up for miles the way we had come to get to where we could switch to another track heading in the general direction of where our command wanted us to go. The Allied bombers had made such a mess of the railroads throughout Germany that it was hit or miss whether we could continue for long in any direction.

The train continued on through Metz, heading toward Nancy, France. That was where we had real trouble. Every railroad around Nancy was in terrible shape and we sat again for long minutes or hours doing nothing, then would travel awhile, stop, and back up to our last stop. It got to the point that every time we came to a stop, men would ask sleepily, "Where we at now?" The answer always came back the same, "Nancy."

This, of course, was not true, but it became a standard answer no matter where we were along our route. We were always just entering Nancy, in Nancy, or just leaving Nancy. A half day's travel later and again we were entering Nancy, in Nancy, or just leaving Nancy. Chuck Gudbrandsen was getting a little more than peeved at this answer— he wanted to know exactly where we were. Gudbrandsen had arrived with us just before Bastogne and had made it this far on his way to becoming one of the older men. I don't recall his ever having been wounded. Maybe he was and I just didn't know about it. It seemed that everyone in our division had been wounded at least once. If you weren't you were a rarity.

Evidently our engineer was informed of another route east and we entered and passed through Sarreguemines, France. We doubled back northward to Homberg, eastward through Kaiserslautern, and on to Ludwigshafen, where our rail trip came to an end on 23 April 1945 after three days cramped in those forty-and-eights with no toilet facilities, stop-and-go travel, and backing up miles to start over. Here we left the train to board DUKWs, amphibious trucks the GIs had nicknamed "Ducks." We picked up our duffel bags from the baggage cars, smuggled the DPs along with us, and boarded the Ducks. We had from twelve to fifteen men on each "Duck," with more room than in the forty-and-eights and a lot smoother ride. We carried our gear and weapons, made ourselves comfortable on board, and settled in for what looked to be a long ride.

There was no layover or waiting; we set out immediately. We moved along the Rhine a little ways. All of the bridges had been destroyed over the Rhine, and for a while we thought our vehicles were going to make an amphibious crossing, but at last we came to a newly constructed American bridge and crossed over into Mannheim. Now in the daylight the Rhine looked muddy gray, not the foreboding inky black it had on the nights we had crossed it before.

We entered onto the autobahn, Hitler's superhighway, and rolled down through Heidelberg, Neckermund, Mosbach, Adelsheim, and Merchingen. At times we came to overpasses on the autobahn that had been destroyed. Their rubble, broken concrete and twisted steel, lay in our path, but the versatile Ducks climbed the banks of the road ramps, skirted the obstacles, rolled down the embankments on the other side, and we continued on with hardly a reduction in speed. At other times bridges had been destroyed directly in the path of our travel, leaving us no alternative but to swim a river, drive back onto the road, and continue on until another obstacle forced us to swim another river or take to a field again.

There were long strips of undamaged highway that were lately being used by the Luftwaffe. Most of their airfields had been destroyed, as had a great many of their vehicles. So the Germans were now taking off and landing what few planes they had left on undamaged and not-too-traveled highways. They had carved out small niches in the trees bordering the improvised "highway runways" where they could store fuel and hide their aircraft until needed. We saw every make of aircraft the Germans had left, including Storches, Me 109s, FW 190s, transports, and a Me 262 jet fighter, all parked along the expressway, armed, fueled, and ready to fly. Just no pilots at this time—the pilots were all heading to the center of their homeland with the rest of the German military.

We were beginning to run into German military stragglers who came out of wherever they had been to walk alongside the autobahn, trying to surrender to someone, anyone. They knew the war was lost. They were tired and hungry. Now they just wanted to go home. We yelled, pointing for them to head back in the direction we had come from. The Americans would feed and care for them back there.

The DUKW convoy pulled into Merchingen, where we again detrucked. A Company was to take up bivouac in a small village just outside Merchingen, where our divisional command post would be billeted. We walked in loose military company formation this time, not strung out in combat formation as we usually did. We marched up a small winding road into town. Just where the road made a final curve before entering town we met a funeral procession coming our way, heading toward a small cemetery we had just passed outside town. Many small children dressed in white and carrying religious symbols led the group. Next came the priest, the coffin, then several people weeping. They in turn were followed by what seemed to be nearly half the population of this small village.

I whispered to my buddies around me that we should stop the funeral and look in the coffin. This town might be burying all their valuables instead of a body, and it was legal to loot from the enemy. We might be passing up a fortune. They were against it and said they doubted if there was anything in the coffin but a body. We should let them bury their dead in peace. I still wanted to open the casket and, if there was a body in it, dump it out on the ground to see what was underneath. In the end we walked around the procession on our way into town, allowing them to go on to the cemetery. Every now and then still I wonder what was really in that coffin. It seemed strange to me that they would have a burial just as we were entering their village for occupation.

Darkness was setting in and we were assigned houses near the center of town. My squad drew first guard duty. As the rest of the company made themselves comfortable, I, as sergeant of the guard, took the 2d Squad around to post them at strategic points, two men to a post. At the far end of the village we came to a group of young teenage civilians who were milling in a group outside several two- and three-story houses.

Boys and girls alike were dressed in black trousers and black wool pullover sweaters. They jeered at us, called us names, and even stepped forward as if to start a brawl. All civilians were to be inside their homes by 8:30 P.M. according to curfew; it was now past that time and dark. I ordered them inside, but they replied in an arrogant, sneering way that we could not force them to obey. Borchers pulled a 9mm pistol and, pointing it at one of the men who seemed to be the ringleader, ordered him into the house. The man stayed leaning against a wall and sneered. A young girl of about seventeen walked up and spat at me, her spittle landing on my chest front.

I was now angry and in no mood to play games. I drew my .45, jammed the muzzle against the nose of the grinning young Nazi ringleader, still leaning with his back against the wall, and slowly cocked the hammer back. He was about my age and about not to get any older. Then I said very quietly, and I meant it, "If you don't get in that house right now and stay there I am going to pull this trigger and blow the top of your head off."

The young Nazi stared at me for a moment. I raised the .45 so that he was looking straight into the barrel. Our eyes met. *"Gross"*— 'big'—he breathed, and closed his eyes, turned, and walked quietly into the house. The rest of the group followed.

On the other side of town we met an older man supposedly getting wood from a small shed across the street from his home. I already knew about guns being hidden in woodpiles. I ordered him back into his house, to get inside and stay there. Anyone caught on the streets after 8:30 P.M. would be shot on sight. He argued with me. Again I pulled the .45, pointed the muzzle between his eyes, and told him the same thing I had just told the young Nazi. His eyes opened, he too muttered, *"Gross,"* and obeyed immediately.

These Nazi people seemed to think they were still the master race, and they could not bring themselves to take orders from non-Germans. The only way to convince them was to use force and be ready and able to kill immediately if they hesitated. Some of them would continue to show defiance when confronted with a smaller-bore pistol or a rifle. But when they looked into the bore of a .45 they immediately obeyed. Several times I heard them mutter, *"Gross, gross;"* the bore of a .45 is big, and it shoots a big bullet.

We made our way in a circuit back toward where we had first entered the village, angled a little to the right, and up a populated hill. I posted two more guard positions with two men on each and started back with Borchers and two other troopers still with me. As we started down the hill, Borchers was walking just to my left. A rifle bullet cracked past my head, nipping my unfastened helmet strap, which hung loosely by my neck. We all turned at once but could not determine which house or window the shot had been fired from. The house in the center of a triangle formed by a Y in the road seemed to be the most likely place. It had a broad view and full command up and down the three streets and into the part of town at the foot of the hill.

We all raced toward it at once. I fired several shots indiscriminately at the windows while one of our men placed himself to cover the front of the house. The other man ran a little farther up the road to our right, where he could watch the rear and most of the surrounding houses as well. I put a bullet through the lock on the door, Borchers kicked it in, and we went inside. We searched through the rooms, even to the third floor, but found no one anywhere; all rooms were empty, vacant of furniture. This was strange in itself, for we had to kick civilians out of houses to make room for ourselves to billet and here was a large three-story house, completely vacant.

Borchers and I each held a grenade with the pins pulled, ready to throw them into rooms if we ran into more trouble than we could handle with rifle and .45. The search revealed no one, so we left the house, looked around several other houses, saw nothing out of the ordinary, and continued on our way.

I made my report to the officer of the day, Lieutenant Borrelli, and started back to the house that billeted my 2d Squad. Music reached my ears. Men were laughing, singing, and having a ball in a large house just up the road from the company CP.

Turning, I walked to the place and entered. Most of A Company men were there drinking and were pretty well on the way. Our combo had gotten together again and with paper-covered comb, pots and pans, and broomstick were turning out what to them must have been beautiful music. Dobrich was singing "Begin the Beguine" at the top of his voice. The only trouble was that he had been singing and drinking for so long that his voice now had the quality of long fingernails being scraped over a school blackboard.

They all invited me in and offered me several bottles at once. What a wonderful opportunity to get totally stoned, but here I was on guard duty and couldn't afford the risk. If some of those young diehard Nazis decided to whoop it up this night, I had better be in a condition to send them on to Valhalla. I did manage a few long drags on the cognac bottle, then returned to the company CP to sit by the radio and wait until guard change.

Nothing of importance happened that night that I was aware of, and the sun rose on a pretty quiet day. In fact the rest of our time here was fairly quiet after our first entrance into town and after the young lions had learned just who was really in command. The young Nazi clique realized after that first encounter that even though we were known as the easygoing and humane Americans, we could also kill if we had to.

The following morning in front of our CP a large map was displayed between two wooden posts. The positions of the Allies' lines were depicted with heavy white cord pinned in place. At one spot the American and Russian lines were closer yet, like two spearheads reaching for each other.

A small group of civilians stood in front of the map, studying the advance of the Allies and the crumbling decay of their own country. The day was 25 April 1945. An officer came out of the command post with a folded paper map in his hand and began moving the string on the larger stationary map. The civilians moved closer to see what new gains we had made. The group grew, women, men, and kids crowding to see what victories and losses had taken place.

The officer finished his work and moved away. A groan came from the civilian group, while yells of victory came from the troopers standing around. The American 69th Division had made contact with the Russian 58th Guards Division on the Elbe River. To us it seemed to be all over but the shouting. Several German women turned toward us, weeping uncontrollably. The older men stood staring blankly at the ground. The two strings representing the U.S. and Russian forces had met, and Germany was cut in half.

# 7 Landsberg

We left Merchingen in the early morning hours of 26 April 1945. After loading up on DUKWs and following highways and roads we could navigate, we started toward the city of Gmünd. Passing through Gmünd this same day, we rolled on toward the city of Ulm, where our convoy would pass over the Danube River. Everyone became interested in the Danube and wanted to see it; we awakened those asleep so they, too, could see it. We had all heard "The Blue Danube" waltz, and we wanted to see for ourselves the beautiful Blue Danube River that had inspired such a world-renowned song.

After traveling from Gmünd we entered Ulm, crossed over an old existing bridge, and looked down at the muddy, swirling waters of the Danube. I have seen drainage ditches in America that were clearer and bluer than that muddy mess. After the men had made their disparaging remarks, most of us lay back to get what sleep we could. One man was heard to say, "When I get back home and hear anyone mention the beautiful 'Blue Danube,' I'll have a word or two for that nitwit."

Our drive began climbing upward—we had arrived at the edge of the German Alps. The air grew colder, and we were running into snows on our way. The ride on the Ducks, being smooth and comfortable, allowed us to sleep or catnap while traveling unopposed through what had been a few days ago a hostile and armed country, now just hostile. The air was cool enough that while traveling we pulled our collars up to protect our faces and necks against the wind and weather.

On leaving Ulm we were headed toward the city of Memmingen. After a time, and before arriving in Memmingen, we pulled into a town and detrucked from the Ducks. We could be spending a few hours or days here; at this point in time no one could say for sure. As it turned out we spent only a few hours, during which we searched for food, wayward Krauts, and weapons. In our searches we found that many retreating German soldiers were still planting pistols, rifles, submachine guns, and ammo near the bottoms of almost every woodpile in almost every town. Since all of Europe was using wood stoves for heat and cooking, they all maintained large woodpiles, which would be all but depleted in the spring. The guns would then be found near the bottom, to be recovered by those Germans using the wood.

We also discovered eggs in crocks of brine stored in basements and sausages hung by strings down chimneys. While we were searching for weapons, Leica cameras, and anything else of value, Borchers, several other troopers, and me were in the third floor attic of a home. Large tobacco leaves were hung to dry on the top ridgepole and other items of value to the family but not to us were also stored. Borchers asked, "What's that small metal door in the chimney for?"

I looked and said, "You guys from big cities like Chicago don't know nothing. That's a cleanout for cleaning the chimney."

"In the top of the chimney," Borchers asked in disbelief.

We pried the metal plate off and saw several wooden pegs set in the bottom portion of the opening, each peg about the size of my forefinger. Attached to the pegs were heavy cords hanging downward. Borchers exclaimed. "I told you. I'll bet there's pistols and all sorts of weapons hanging in there."

We pulled on the cords and up came sausage after sausage tied end to end on each cord, all hanging down the chimney to smoke while the woodstove heated the house. Running downstairs we showed the others, telling them where we had found them. Word spread quickly through the small town and soon A Company had stores of smoked sausages, cold-storage eggs, schnapps, and cognac for out trip into the Alps. A great change from K rations. During our short stay in this small town we ate and drank well and some men even had the bonus of becoming owners of expensive cameras and other objects of value. "Articles of War. Looting from an enemy is legal."

Orders to move out sounded; we loaded our sausages and other loot on board our DUKWs, picked spots to ride in, and headed out. The last thing I took from the house was a fur collar I ripped from a woman's cloth coat hanging on the wall near the front door. As we rode I took the small sewing kit from my musette bag and sewed the fur to the collar of my combat jacket. With the collar turned up, the fur kept the cold wind from my face and neck.

The 506th entered Memmingen on 27 April 1945, pigtailing the 44th Division, which had captured the city the day before. Prisoner-of-war camps lay scattered all about the area and the 44th Division had the honor and privilege of liberating many hundreds of Allied prisoners of war from these camps. It seemed the 101st was now relegated to mopping up for other divisions that had better modes of transportation than did the airborne and were able to race on ahead. With the war's end in sight all military units wanted to be in on the kill, and the race was on to see which division would have the honor of being the first to enter Hitler's Eagle Nest, Berchtesgaden.

While units of the 101st Airborne Division stayed on in Memmingen and Kaufburen, the 506th Regiment received orders to help the 4th Division capture the city of Landsberg. Early in the morning of 28 April 1945 the 506th moved out of Memmingen aboard Ducks, passed through Kaufburen, and headed eastward in the direction of Landsberg.

Our road carried us up, down, and along the sides of hills. The scenery was beautiful, with snow-covered mountains ahead. Signs of war in villages and cities diminished the farther we went into the Alps, passing over roads without stopping or slowing. The sun was shining bright as we traveled. After some time we began a descent down a mountainside on a long, winding road. We could see in the distance a huge billow of black oily smoke rising from the valley floor to scar the sight of beautiful snowy mountains and clear blue sky. Our orders to help the 4th Division in taking the city of Landsberg would be our first real combat action in quite a while. It would probably be a tough battle, or why else would anyone request the aid of the 101st Airborne Division?

As we came down a long grade, with hills to our left, we could see some sort of large camp below to our right. It seemed hours before we reached the flatland and went racing toward the center of town, passing to the left of the large camp we had seen from the mountainside. A long building nearest the side of the road we traveled was enveloped in flames. Still not knowing the situation or what lay ahead, our convoy slowed as the road leveled. To our right we viewed what appeared to be large warehouses and rows of barracks, all standing behind a high heavy cyclone-style wire fence that continued around a large military complex. Continuing at a slower pace, we entered Landsberg. We came to another area that was enclosed with a high wire fence topped with rolls of barbed wire. Behind the fence was a sight I will never forget: bodies upon bodies of starved, skeletal human beings. They were piled about three feet or higher in a mass that seemed to cover the largest part of this side of the compound. Living skeletons dressed in blue-and-white-striped uniforms wandered about in the streets and within the compound; others just stood inside the wire enclosure like zombies, staring without seeing. Some of our Ducks slowed to a lower gear and drove through the high fence. Staples popped, wires stretched taut and broke, whistling as they whipped through the air.

Our convoy came to a stop and we dismounted. We could go no farther: the bridge across the Lech River had been destroyed. We surveyed the wreckage. Fast-running water ran through twisted steel beams and broken concrete of all sizes. Stumps of the main bridge supports stood among the rubble. There was no way we could cross even with the amphibious DUKWs. If we continued east we would have to locate a place where the DUKWs could enter, cross, and leave the river safely.

A bullet smashed into a wall of a building behind us, followed by the sound of a shot. Someone across the river was sniping at us. It wasn't a trained sniper, or one of our men would have been killed—snipers don't miss. We tried to locate the probable spot he was shooting from, but to no avail. Troopers began firing into windows and other openings in the houses across the Lech River in hopes of killing the shooter or spooking him into revealing himself. Minutes later, after a lot of guesswork on our side, came another shot that also missed. This was embarrassing, for we could not spot the sniper and we could not move freely about, even with a bad marksman.

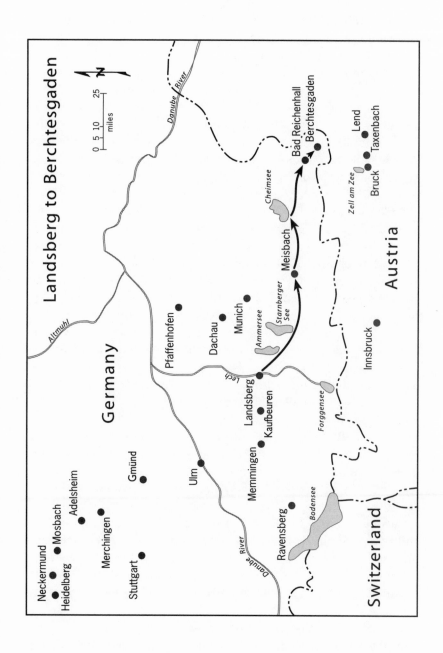

Someone yelled, "I see him, I know where he's at." And he pointed to a window in a house across the river. It was a long shot and the walls were thick. It would be a miracle if one of us could hit him.

"Just a minute," another trooper said. "I know where there's a Sherman tank, I'll get him." The man took off running back down the road we had entered on. Within minutes he returned with a tank following him, the main gun pointing upward and ready. The trooper pointed to the window in the third floor of a house facing us. The tank maneuvered, adjusted its main battery, and fired. The whole upper front of the house, along with the roof, blew apart in wreckage. There was no more shooting from that side of the river.

Unknown to us at that moment was that our American 4th Infantry Division, along with the 10th Armored Division, had entered the city of Landsberg the evening before our arrival. We had been ordered to help the 4th Division take this city, but things were moving fast now, and the Germans weren't putting up the last-ditch struggle that had been expected. It all came down to animal instinct. The Germans were no longer fighting for the Fatherland; they were trying to stay alive to return home, now that they realized their war was lost. Facing little resistance, all Allied units were moving as fast as they could to be in on that last kill. The others would not wait for us and had left to join the race without seeing to the needs of the inmates of the Landsberg concentration camp.

Most inmates appeared near death, walking skeletons. A few who were in slightly better condition than the others came stumbling, holding their arms out to us, wanting to embrace, to thank us for their liberation. As much compassion as we felt for them we just couldn't bring ourselves to accept their hugs, for they looked near death, had dysentery caked down their legs, large open sores on their arms and legs, and they looked as though they might have had lice and other vermin. Our medics and others went to fetch help, returning a short time later with a group of nuns. I think they were nuns. They wore full ground-length, dark-blue dresses with white caps that had starched cloth gull-like wings sticking outward on either side.

Immediately they began caring for these poor miserable creatures we had just liberated, carrying some into what appeared to be an infirmary, others to huts that had beds. A few in critical condition were made to lie on the ground where they were, to be made as comfortable as possible with blankets in their last moments of life. Many smiled as they passed on, knowing they had died in freedom.

Troopers were wandering freely about the camp. Carl Angelly, Harold Phillips, Leonard Benson, and I entered some of the buildings, hardly believing what we saw there. The whole camp was one large torture camp. Inmates, as we later learned from the prisoners, had been strapped to tables and dissected while alive and aware, without the benefit of any anesthetics whatsoever. In one room that was evidently a filthily kept, crude operating room with a wood-framed operating table, I saw where spurts of living blood had sprayed dotted and solid streams up the walls and across the ceiling. Blood covered the four walls as high as our shoulders. Slaughterhouses in the States weren't this messy and blood spattered. We found it hard to accept. I visualized naked victims fastened to the table with the heavy medical restraining straps lying on the floor at our feet and while conscious having a "doctor," oblivious to their screams and pleas for mercy, methodically cut them apart, one bit at a time.

Moving to the back wall, I readied my rifle and kicked a door open. Inside was a shoulder-high pile of prostheses, artificial arms and legs of all sorts. What had happened here? I kicked another door open. There on a table was the naked body of a young woman who had attempted to give birth. Heavy restraining straps had been bound tight around her legs and thighs. The same type of straps had also held her to the table in a fetal position. White-painted wooden kitchen-style chairs were set in a semicircle around the table for an audience that evidently had sat watching this woman die in agony attempting to give an impossible birth. I looked at her face, the bulged eyes, her open mouth. She had died screaming her lungs out.

I didn't know what to do. I wanted to take my trench knife and cut her bonds. What good would that do? Phillips, Angelly, and Benson had entered behind me. They stood saying nothing. We turned and left the room.

Outside we interviewed women who were able to walk and associate with others. We asked questions; they answered candidly. The women prisoners had many tales to tell, too many and too morbid to relate in total. The women were constantly subjected to a variety of methods of sterilization. Some were bombarded in the belly area at close range with X rays for different time periods, then strapped to the operating table, where they were subjected to a complete hysterectomy without the aid of anesthetics. The "doctors" would then be able to view the effects of the X ray and the other methods used. After the operation the "patient" was stitched up and allowed to make her way outside, where she would get on her hands and knees and crawl backward into one of a row of doghouse-like shelters and lie down. There she would stay to survive on her own, or die. Once a woman died, other women would scavenge the clothes from her body.

I inquired of the prostheses I had seen in one of the small buildings. Several women told of men wearing artificial arms or legs, who from time to time came to this camp. They, too, were fastened to the operating table, where "doctors" removed the prostheses. Then, with scalpels, probes, hooks, and other surgical instruments, they would cut, probe, and hook nerve and muscle endings and pull them out from the living stump. There they examined the healed body parts, muscles, and nerve and bone endings to determine how well the healing had been.

The Germans had many of their own returning with missing limbs, and these "doctors" evidently felt they would gain knowledge by this manner of study to aid them. Once a complete "examination" had taken place, none of the patients survived. Crematoriums, mass graves, and holding pits took care of the butchered cadavers.

Troopers roamed freely within the camp, not in orderly fashion but at random or out of morbid curiosity; and in the hope of finding a hiding Nazi prison guard who had been too dumb to leave and had been overlooked by others. Civilian authorities and others had been rounded up in town, MPs had arrived, orders given, and responsibility delegated to those who could be held accountable.

A Company moved left along the road that ran alongside the river. Other troops moved in the opposite direction. A large building stood near the main corners to our left front facing the Lech River. This building turned out to be a telegraph, post office, and bank building combination. Here we were told to billet ourselves. In one of the lower rooms stood hundreds of Nazi swastika flags, lying flat in stacks waist high along a wall, all new and ready for placement on German vehicles. They were convoy flags, commonly used on their vehicles for identification. I took one, folded it, and stuffed it in one of my leg cargo pockets as a souvenir. We hadn't quite settled in when our company commander, First Lieutenant Kennedy, asked. "Why should my men sleep in an empty office building while the enemy sleeps in warm houses?"

Lieutenant Kennedy ordered us into formation and appropriated houses for each platoon and squad to billet in until further notice. The house our 2d Squad drew was a large brick-and-stone two-story place at the farthest end to the left of our billet area. We had to wait while a young German woman, weeping heavily, holding a baby and pulling a small wagon loaded with clothing, left the house. Once gone, she was under strict orders not to return for any reason until after we had left.

Another squad of A Company occupied the house next to us, closer to the center of Landsberg, but I don't recall just who it was. Angelly and I moved quickly to the second floor. We had learned in the past that most of the men would run about the first floors trying to get the best sleeping spots, and only then would the ones who hadn't done well take to the second floor. Angelly and I claimed a large bed and placed our helmets and rolls on it. Then we began searching for mementos to liberate.

The house was filled with souvenirs from the States. Small statuettes of the Statue of Liberty were among the many items that didn't interest us. A small wood-burning stove stood in the center of a large luxurious living room, or parlor, in which a couple of troopers were attempting to start a fire. "Get some paper," one of them yelled. We looked through the closets and found a bundle about twenty inches cubic of German marks tightly bound with baling wire. After some attempts with bayonets and other knives we finally managed to open the "treasure" and found mark notes of high denomination, up to several million marks per note.

We actually thought we were rich, until we noticed the dates on the bills. It was inflation money from after World War I, and had no use except the one we put it to, starting the fire. We took pleasure in pawing through the pile of money on the floor to see who could find the largest-denomination notes—five million marks, I think—and throw them into the stove to watch them burn.

Angelly and I had walked into the kitchen to prepare our K rations the best we could, when a chicken cackled in the backyard announcing that she had just laid an egg. Carl and I looked at each other and ran for the stairs. As we burst from the doorway, running across the backyard toward the chicken coop, we saw a man from the house next door also running for the same coop, which was on our side of the fence. He evidently had a spot on his first floor and so had a head start on us. He leapt the fence, opened the coop door, and grabbed the egg, proudly holding it aloft in triumph on his way back to his house. "I got the egg," he said, grinning. Angelly reached into the coop, grabbed the hen, wrung its neck, and holding it up said, "Yeah, and we got the chicken." Back in our house we cooked the chicken to supplement our K rations and shared it with the rest of our squad.

After eating we walked back toward the center of town, to the large fenced-in concentration camp which stood close to the Landsberg Prison building, where in 1923 Hitler had been imprisoned and wrote his first draft of *Mein Kampf.* Arriving at the camp, we found that other troopers, along with the drivers of the Ducks, had driven their vehicles through the high fence in several places, opening more holes. Once more the inmates wanted to hug us and give their thanks in appreciation for our liberation of their camp. Again we declined their embraces, maneuvering away from them in another direction. We climbed aboard the Ducks to avoid these people; they were too weak to climb after us. One trooper came to us and said he had just given a chocolate bar to an older man begging for food. The inmate bolted the chocolate down and shortly went into convulsions and died writhing at the trooper's feet. The trooper was visibly shaken. He said he hadn't meant to kill the man, he was only trying to be helpful. These people had been surviving on potato-peeling soup for years and were walking skeletons. Their systems would not accept rich food, especially chocolate.

Climbing down from the Ducks, we made our way into the camp. Skeletal bodies were in piles and stacked everywhere. They weren't stacked neatly in rows as an undertaker might have done the job; they were thrown in huge piles in a haphazard manner. All were naked, having been stripped of clothing by their fellow inmates. Some were badly burned. When they had heard of our approach they had barricaded themselves in barracks, refusing to come out when ordered to do so by the SS. The SS in turn set fire to the barracks, then machine-gunned the inmates when at last they sought to escape the flames. Attempts had been made by guards, before our arrival, to bury the dead in mass graves, in large trenches gouged out of the earth by bulldozers and in craters blown out of the ground by explosives. There were too many bodies. All but a few guards had fled.

Sitting atop one large pile of bodies we saw a withered old creature, rocking back and forth sideways, softly moaning, or was it humming? We got closer; the pitiful form turned out to be a woman, nearly naked but in such terrible shape that it was all but impossible to tell if she were male or female until we got close to her. Her breasts were merely two pieces of withered skin lying flat against an extended rib cage. Another woman who was in better condition and spoke fragmentary English told me that the moaning creature's husband had died a few days before and was lying somewhere in the mass of rotting cadavers and that the woman didn't want to leave him. I listened to the soft sounds of her crooning and the hair crawled up the back of my neck. She was singing to her dead husband.

The stench was terrible. The smell of decaying human bodies, along with that of human excrement and vomit, was like a thick, heavy abominable oil that penetrated every particle of air. One could not help but breathe it, even taste it, and for the first time I saw some battle-hardened troopers get sick.

My God, you could smell this place for miles, and once a person experienced that odor he would never forget it. One could even see the inside of the camp from the street—the wretched beings inside being reduced to animals, then rotting bodies. How could anyone honestly say they didn't know? At times walking through the compound, the smell became so thick I would have to fight the retching, constricting muscles in my stomach to keep from vomiting.

Inmates in the familiar blue-and-white-striped suits were wandering out into the streets. The healthier DPs wandered in packs, like animals. They invaded German homes, taking what they wanted—food, clothes, bicycles, anything they could carry off. Some set about trying to beat German civilians but were too weak to do it. The Germans were afraid to protest or say anything for fear we would take reprisals against them. One frail DP woman entered a German house and emerged carrying a treadle sewing machine on her head. She staggered and swayed under its weight but did not drop it. She wandered aimlessly up and down the street with it balanced on her head. The heavy machine must have had some significance for her. I felt sure she would drop it sooner or later, but the next day when I saw her again she was still carrying it on her head everywhere.

A group of us, including Angelly, Borchers, Surface, Hull, Benson, and others walked farther into the camp to survey what had been going on here away from the civilized world. We came to the ovens, still belching black oily smoke. Some of the inmates who had been delegated by the SS guards to put the bodies of their own comrades into the ovens were still stoking the fires with bodies. We stopped them in their chores. They stood as vacuous as zombies, not knowing what to do, fearful of being punished for not working.

Every oven had a set of metal tracks about belt high leading into the door, much like streetcar tracks, on which they could lay a metal stretcher to hold a human body. These metal stretchers were affixed with metal clasps at the corners to hold those who weren't dead as yet and tried to fight their way off. One man on each door was assigned to examine the cadavers' mouths to find any gold that might have been overlooked just before they were slid along the tracks into the flames. It was his job to pry the gold out and drop it into a small metal can set in a wire hoop fastened alongside the door opening. The gold teeth were gathered from these cans periodically by guards who made regular rounds of the ovens. More piles of bodies were at the entrance of each oven, while DPs dragged yet more bodies in to add to the pile, until we stopped them also.

Taking my rifle barrel, I opened the hot doors of several ovens. Inside I saw that the fire in most had consumed all or most of the bodies. A few ovens had larger bones, like the pelvis, the large leg bones, or a skull still on the grates. This room of bodies with gaping mouths and sunken eyes, along with the overpowering odor, was beginning to get to us, and we wandered toward the main gate. On the way we stopped in the guards' quarters, where we witnessed patches of tattooed human skin tacked on the walls and several lamps with tattooed human skin dried to form lampshades. At first we didn't know what they were, then recognition set in. These were souvenirs none of us cared to take along with us.

In the main compound troopers were ordering Germans in uniform to carry the bodies to burial holes and cover them over with lime and dirt in a gesture of decent interment. We felt it fitting that these Germans be made to handle the corpses with bare hands, though some begged for gloves to wear at this chore. This went on until runners came into the compound telling everyone that the latest orders were not to bury any more bodies. There were aircraft bearing newsmen and photographers coming in and they wanted to photograph and make movie films to document these horrors and atrocities before any more burials.

A little later Gen. Maxwell D. Taylor, commander of the 101st Airborne Division, ordered all civilians in Landsberg to assemble in the concentration camp to view the corpses, to see how they had been tortured and murdered. We had also found, in the hills, large pits, at the bottoms of which surplus bodies had been carted and dumped in huge piles awaiting cremation. Other bodies were scattered along the pathway to the pits, evidently dropped by the laborers hauling them when they learned of our approach.

The civilians of Landsberg we forced to spend the day in the hills viewing the bodies. They were allowed to come down just before dark. Two young teenage girls came down the path laughing and making jokes while they walked. General Taylor, infuriated, made them go back up to spend the night among the pits of cadavers. The next morning they came down shaking and weeping uncontrollably.

Further orders from General Taylor had the citizens of Landsberg—men, women, and children—show up the next morning with rakes, shovels, and brooms to clean up the areas and to take bodies down from the pits for burial. The filming and photography, along with interviews with those who could give testimony, had been completed; it was time to care for the dead. The two young German girls who had laughed the day before as if this were some lark were put to work carrying cadavers. They both began vomiting so violently that they had to rest alongside the road until they were able to resume work.

These civilians were to continue in these chores until all was cleaned up and traces of the carnage were removed. They also had to help the DPs with clothing and in any other manner they could.

This presented another problem. Most of the DPs had been left more or less to fend for themselves the first day. Now we had the chore of bringing some semblance of control and order to the area. We more or less dragged them from German homes, where they had been helping themselves to whatever they wanted, and herded them into a large group in the compound. Most did not want to return, and we had to—under orders—fix bayonets and drive them into the compound, where leaders of Jews, Poles, Czechs, Russians, and others who had been prisoners would help us guide them to showers and clean clothing.

Each leader explained in his own language what was happening and what was to be expected. It was a chore to get them to the open-ended shower shed that was set up by our engineers, but by talking, threats, and shoving we finally managed to get a group to undress and enter the hot shower. They were handed GI soap, the hot water was turned on, and they began loosening up to enjoy their first real bath in many months, if not years.

Then, just as the first group was leaving by the open rear of the shower room, several medics sitting on either side with large canisters of DDT began spraying the freshly showered people to rid them of vermin. This was all similar to the way the Nazis had exterminated thousands of victims before them. They were too close to freedom and life now to give up. They went hysterical, *"Gaz, Gaz, Gaz,"* they cried. They were immediately a wild, howling mob of animals. They fought like maniacs. We had a real job subduing them, but when it was finally done we showed them that we, too, would allow ourselves to be "gassed," and DDT was sprayed freely on us in turn.

Two of our medics, along with two DP leaders, took off their clothing and walked into the shower together as the people nervously watched. On exiting the shower at the far end the medics held their arms high, turning around while other medics, using nozzled hoses attached to the large metal canisters of DDT, sprayed the men's bodies thoroughly.

Soon a couple of DPs, in the company of the two medics, cautiously went through the shower and the DDT ritual and received fresh laundered clothing on the other side. On seeing this, others—men, women, boys, and girls—crowded to the showers, the delousing, and the fresh new clothes. Afterward a hot meal of weakened food, (thinned vegetable soup with a little meat) was served in large mess halls that had once belonged to the German soldiers. The final phase we were to help with was the grouping of the DPs into Jews, Poles, Czechs, Russians, and so on, and assigning them to former German barracks. Married couples were placed in billets in the center barracks of each block, with single men at one end of the block and single girls at the other. Spokespersons were selected in each group to be in charge of each barrack. These in turn would voice the requests of the people in their care to a head committee made up of a representative from each ethnic group.

Our military was still in command overall, in a diplomatic sort of way. We did not order the DPs around, but rather tried to convey our wishes through their committee. Everything worked out well once we understood each other, and soon medical examinations and help were administered and special needs attended to.

The men of my squad stood in the compound, which had been fairly cleaned by now and the bodies removed. We witnessed a group of Jews coming toward us, heading in the direction of the river, where grass was beginning to green a little. Men carried a metal stretcher between them, staggering under the weight, with women and weaker men following. Something piled on the stretcher was covered with a dark purple cloth. Curiosity led us to approach and examine the cargo. It was soap, large cakes of yellow laundry soap.

We stood dumbfounded. Why would a people so weakened as to be near death be carrying a large supply of laundry soap? We asked the ones following. They told us this was soap made of the rendered fat of human beings. The German camp guardians had been rendering human bodies—Russian, Poles, and Jews—for fat to make laundry soap, which was then distributed to German civilians. This soap was buried with ceremony in a hole that had been previously dug near the center of a large space of grass.

Our work done, my companions and I walked to the prison where Hitler had been imprisoned. On entering the large front entrance we found a foyer with a fairly large room to the left and what appeared to be a smaller room to the right. The walls of this smaller room were hidden by file cabinets. Indeed, perhaps this room was not smaller than the other, but was only made to seem so by the file cabinets. An older man, who by dress and facial hair appeared to be a rabbi, was bent over trays on a table he had removed from the cabinets. We approached with respect, asking if he knew the cell where Hitler had spent his jail time here.

He continued his search for a moment or two. Then, looking at us, he directed us to climb the stairway to the second floor and take the hall to the right. The cell we were looking for would be near the end on the right. We thanked him but, before leaving, asked what he was up to. The old man replied that these were the records of everyone who had entered the Landsberg Prison and that he was now in charge of them. He asserted, in effect, that he was going to see that they would not be destroyed and that they would be recorded for future use.

We continued upstairs and turned right down a hallway, which curved back around to our left. Near the end on the right-hand side we located what we thought to be the correct cell. Only, it didn't look like a jail cell back home. This was roomier, more like a small hotel room, with a large window, writing table, dresser, and wardrobe—very clean and comfortable. There was no sign or other evidence that this was Hitler's actual cell, only the word of the man downstairs in the small record office. There were, however, holes in the wall over the door where a sign had recently been ripped away by a souvenir seeker or a disgruntled DP. That bronze sign has never been recovered. It read as follows:

HERE A DISHONORABLE SYSTEM IMPRISONED GERMANY'S GREATEST SON FROM NOVEMBER 11, 1923, TO DECEMBER 20, 1924.

During that time and in this very cell Adolf Hitler wrote his book of the "National Socialist Revolution," *Mein Kampf* (My Struggle).

Later that night it suddenly dawned on me that this older man, the rabbi, had been dressed in black, complete with black hat, and had a beard. All Jews and other inmates I ever saw in these camps at this time wore the blue-and-white-striped uniforms, had their heads shaved, were half starved, and none ever had a beard. Years later I still wonder if the man had really been a rabbi or was someone pretending to be one in order to remove certain records before a real rabbi came along.

On leaving the Landsberg Prison we made our way back through some of the buildings surrounding the concentration-camp compound. In one large building we discovered bales of human hair. The bales were the same size and shape as a hay or straw bale would be and might even have been put up with a hay-baling machine. The bales were stacked as high as the ceiling. Contained in the bale we could see large swatches of dark hair, blond, gray, and other colors. All prisoners who entered these camps had their heads shaved, both men and women, but this was the first evidence of what happened to that hair. Just what the Germans used it for, I don't know, but in total there must have been several tons of hair gathered and baled at each camp.

We met women inmates who by now had cleaned up, had been issued clean clothing, and had eaten their first good meals in several years. It is amazing how fast some begin to bounce back to recovery after a horrible, prolonged ordeal. These people were just starting out again. They had a long way to go. We talked with those who could speak our language and they in turn translated to those who didn't. Some of the women had spent time at a nearby camp at Ravensberg and for reasons unknown had been transferred here. Perhaps Ravensberg had no crematorium, as did Landsberg. They told us of the tortures and the attempts at mass- and cheap-sterilization experiments carried out there. Many of these women would never bear children as a result of those experiments. The doctors there had also performed operations and experiments without administering anesthetics. The "patients" were strapped down and operated on, then released to recover on their own, if they could.

One such hideous operation had been recorded in writing and on film. The Germans were concerned about their pilots who were shot down over the English Channel and at sea. Most died of hypothermia after a short immersion in the cold water. The doctors took a male inmate, dressed him in a rubberized suit complete with a tight-fitting hood, and placed him in a large vat with water at thirty-five degrees Fahrenheit.

He was forced to stay shoulder deep in this water until he showed signs of severe hypothermia, then was removed, undressed, and strapped to the operating table. The doctors cut and sawed the top of his skull off, exposing the brain and discarding the skullcap and scalp. The man was still alive and conscious but helpless to move. The doctors cut and probed veins and small arteries to see the effects of hypothermia on the blood supply system in a living brain. In the end the brain was completely destroyed and the man dead.

We were told of brutalities and tortures at the hands of prison guards—of how men, women, and children were made to stand naked in the freezing cold and were hosed down with water. How many of the young women who were still filled out and shapely were taken to German quarters to serve at the pleasure of the Nazis. I could not fathom any human being treating another in such a way. I could kill, yes, but never treat anyone as these people had been treated.

It was simpler to sterilize men than women. They were castrated with a knife and turned loose to see if they could still run and how far. Some were shot with pistols as they ran, or on the spot where they fell. Their bodies were stripped of clothing, thrown on a cart, and hauled away by inmates to be dumped into large pits until they could be "processed."

We could not begin to imagine some of the stories of other experiments, of chemical injections into the bodies and veins of victims, blood transfusions with animals, and whatever else the twisted mind could conjure up. On tables we also found evidence of wine-stained tops of human skulls from which young SS men had used to drink to prove their manhood.

We left the compound, walking back up the road along which we had entered Landsberg, back to the German barracks and the large warehouses we had seen on our way in. Displaced persons making their way into Landsberg from other places had taken up residence in the former German barracks, each group establishing its own little section or ghetto of Jews, Poles, Russians, Czechs, and others. All were bettering themselves, gathering strength, and making ready for the day when they could start back home.

It is difficult to comprehend how some could have started anew. They had seen their children gassed, their families tortured and worked to death, and in the end all were starved and treated as lower than animals. How could one find the heart to start over?

We spoke to nearly all we met. They in turn thanked us for their rescue, their freedom.

Arriving at the warehouses and entering, we just stood in amazement. There, contained within the walls, was nearly every weapon of war ever invented and manufactured. Rows and rows of cannons of all types and vintage one could imagine, from huge ancient ones with large iron wheels from which metal spikes protruded to new modern cannon. Mortars of every size and description. Machine guns from ancient to modern. Piles of rifles, bayonets, swords, daggers, knives, and pistols—on and on. We found weapons in amounts and of a description we had never dreamed of. All these weapons were the spoils of war Germany had gleaned from every country they had conquered, all brought here and stored in massive warehouses in Landsberg, Germany.

A couple of our troopers took a small carbine, each with folding bayonet, as novelties. We spent the rest of the day looking through and mentally cataloging what item we wanted from the mountainous horde of weaponry that we would take with us on our way out. As always, whether wading through weapons on a battlefield or in a warehouse, we didn't pick up a single item. When we were ready to leave, we simply walked away, leaving all behind.

Back at our billet we had chow; we were sitting as a squad in the large luxurious living room when Borchers walked in with a smirk on his face. "What are you up to?" I asked.

"Nothing," Borchers replied.

When we all went back to passing the schnapps around and telling stories, Borchers suddenly pulled a small tommy gun from under his jacket and shot an entire magazine of bullets across a large oil painting on the wall. The tommy gun was an exact copy of the American tommy gun in every respect, to the smallest detail, only it fired a .25-caliber bullet. The darned little thing was less than half the length and size of our regular tommy gun. Everyone wanted one and wanted to know just where Borchers had picked this one up.

Borchers said he had found it in the large warehouse we had just left and hadn't seen another like it anywhere. This one he was going to keep to take back to the States when the war was over. Most of the men left to go back and search the warehouses, but none found another like the one Borchers had.

That night some of my platoon was on guard in the Russian compound. We pulled two hours on, four off. When the first men came back to the company area, they told us we should visit with the Russians. Phillips, Angelly, Benson, a couple of other troopers, and I walked up the hill and greeted the Russians, who were gathered hunched around a fire. They welcomed us into their midst and offered us bowls of hot vodka out of five-gallon tins from which the tops had been cut out, all set close to the fire to heat. It was snowing when we'd started up here, and now it was coming down harder, with an accumulation of a couple inches on the ground. The Russians stood around stripped to the waist, drinking and laughing loudly.

One Russian patted me on the shoulder and asked if I were an *"Unteroffizier,"* to which I replied, *"Da."*

"Comrade, comrade," he exclaimed, then dipped a heavy white porcelain bowl, hand and all, into the hot vodka, brought it up dripping, and offered it to me. He took a long drink from it first, then handed it to me. Several other Russians watched, grinning, as I accepted his offer, turned it up, and sipped delicately. The stuff was like battery acid and nearly tore the lining from my throat. The name *vodka* was a misnomer—this homemade stuff was anything but vodka, but that is what our Russian hosts called it.

The Russians howled with glee as I sputtered and coughed. The man who had given me the bowl said something in his own language, which I knew to be "Bottoms up." Then his eyes glinted in the firelight as he leaned close into my face, repeating the phrase.

I turned the bowl up and drained it. It seemed minutes before I could catch my breath as the big Russian slapped my shoulder yelling, "Comrade, comrade." He took the porcelain cereal-sized bowl and dipped it back into the large tin, clear to the bottom, and came up with the vodka running down his arm and dripping off his elbow. Again he handed me the bowl and I drained it in one long draft.

Several of the Russians began singing, and others joined in, as I watched the snow hit their naked bodies, melt, and run in small rivulets of water down their reddened skin which glistened in the firelight. I was caught up with the wild melody of their singing and picked up another bowl from the snow, dipped it in the can, and drank again. Wanting to join in their singing and not knowing the words, I hummed along. I threw off my overcoat, then my combat jacket, and by now was humming very loudly. The cold wind and ice hit me like a shower from the arctic. I put my combat jacket back on, buttoning it to the top, put my overcoat back on, fastening it all the way up, turned up the collar, and walked with Phillips, Angelly, and Benson away from there, back to the warmth of the kitchen stove awaiting us in our billet.

# 8 Berchtesgaden

On 1 May 1945 we moved out of our billets and boarded a collection of DUWKs and other assorted transports, including German military and civilian vehicles. We made our way north to Augsberg, then swung back down to Starnberg. Starnberg was a quiet place, not at all like the hellhole we had just left. There was practically no evidence of war except for the abandoned German equipment strewn along the roadsides. Much of the equipment was in good operational condition but out of fuel. This gave evidence to the haste in which the once proud Nazi forces were withdrawing; they couldn't take the time to scrounge fuel for all their vehicles.

We chose the houses and the sleeping arrangements we wanted, then set out to look for hidden weapons and possibly a Kraut who was hiding from forced military service so near to the end of the war. No one really wanted to be one of the last casualties of a lost war. I didn't want to be one of the last casualties of a war won. Our second squad entered one of the many labor camps we had been liberating along the way. These labor camps differed from the concentration camps in that the Germans kept and fed these laborers better, as draft animals, than they did the prisoners in the concentration camps where the prisoners were starved, tortured, killed, and cremated. The laborers were used for road and railroad work, along with being rented out to farmers as field hands and to factories as workers. The farmers and factories would pay the officials of the labor camps to rent these laborers, the profit supposedly going to the German government. The camp officials also charged the factories and farmers for the laborers' meals, which the camp supplied. But

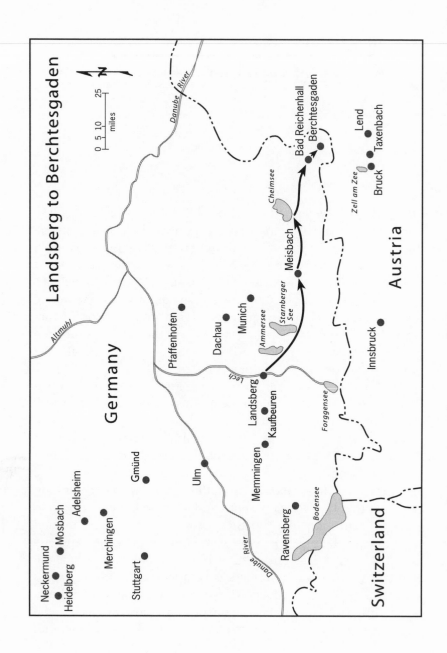

Landsberg to Berchtesgaden

who kept the records and just how much of the profit of the labor rentals actually went to the government?

The camp we entered was clean, the barracks built well against cold weather, and a large building near the front entrance was set aside for social gatherings by the prisoners. In these camps the inmates told us that most of the guards weren't too rough on them and even joined in some of their get-togethers at Christmastime and other holidays.

This was also true in a small POW camp we liberated in a back part of some mountain area close by. Here Australians who had been captured at the very beginning of the war inhabited the entire camp. We visited with them for an afternoon. They were well fed and their quarters were well built, weatherproof, clean, had beds and heating stoves, and weren't as bad as some of the American army camps I had stayed in.

They were all preparing to leave, and most of them had more legal loot than we did. Where and how they had managed to get it I don't know and didn't ask. One of them had large binoculars that he was packing in a box with paper so they wouldn't be damaged traveling. They had cameras and told us they had been allowed to keep their cameras and watches all the way through captivity. They had also been allowed to put on stage shows and handed us photos of some of the plays they had mounted, complete with costumes and wigs.

The man packing the binoculars said the only time they'd had it rough was just a week before our arrival. The SS had arrived unannounced for a surprise inspection and made them all stand at rigid attention alongside their bunks. During the walk-through one of the SS men would stop in front of an inmate and beat him in the face with his fist, then crush the next man's foot under his steel-clad boot. The SS destroyed personal property and gave the impression that they were going to take everyone outside and shoot them.

The regular guards finally tried to intervene, but they, too, were struck and beaten by the SS. In the end one young SS man stopped in front of the Aussie who was now packing the binoculars, noticed he had a gold watch and chain, and tore it from his pocket. The Aussie protested, saying that it belonged to his father and the regular guards had allowed him to keep it all these years. The SS trooper dropped the watch to the floor and crushed it under his steel boot heel, then turned and walked out.

In another camp not too far from this one, hidden under a heavy growth of green pines, we found another POW camp. This one had held American airmen, from the evidence we could see, but no one was here, German or American. The place was built of rough-sawn lumber with only the outer walls in place, no inside covering like wallboard or plaster. The lumber's edges hadn't been trimmed or planed, so when it was nailed to the outer wall large cracks or openings showed between the planking, which allowed bugs to enter in the summer and snow to blow through in the winter.

We found Red Cross boxes in the guards' quarters, which had been torn open and emptied. The prisoners' quarters were Spartan. The beds were too short, with a little hay or straw to sleep on, no mattress covers, and I saw no blankets. It gets cold in the winter in the Alps. I wondered how long, how many years, these American airmen had had to endure this harsh treatment.

Along the way we had been losing our transports back to the units we had originally borrowed them from. We had to make do with vehicles discarded by the retreating Germans. We worked on them, got them in running order, obtained fuel for them, and added them to our ever-growing gypsy caravan. Our motorcade was made up of everything that would roll—Volkswagens, buses, trucks, half-tracks, Mercedes-Benzes, armored cars, motorcycles, and so on, and those that were roomy but wouldn't run, we towed behind other vehicles that did run.

In these years the airborne had little in the way of transportation. A few jeeps that could be flown in by glider to be used by our artillery units, medics, and our higher command—that was about the limit of our motor pool. During training in England we were forced to hire civilian buses with English civilian drivers to haul us to where we needed to go, if we weren't jumping in and the distance was too far to be practical to hike on foot.

During heavy battles, if we needed transportation, other units were only too happy to loan us trucks, Ducks, jeeps, or anything else required to get us to the battle area where we would do the fighting.

But now that the war was in its last stages, with little fighting or re-sistance from the enemy, it was another story. All other units, re-gardless if they were transportation, keepers of warehouses, or just plain rear echelon, wanted to be in on the kill and took back their trucks, Ducks, jeeps, and whatever else they had loaned us, leaving us afoot to get along the best way we could.

The major part of my platoon was assigned a rickety old German civilian bus that was thought to be ready for the trip through the mountains. We took our place in the convoy and started up the long, grueling roadways. O'Neal was driving. The Alps were beautiful, with snowcapped mountains, forests, and winding roads, but we could not relax our vigil; the war was still on. Each man carried his weapons at the ready as always, from habit. If an ambush occurred, it would be at close range and we would be in a bad situation all packed aboard buses. We stuck close, one vehicle to another, in our advance toward Berchtesgaden.

Our going up was a slow, grinding affair, but after we hit the crest of a ridge of high mountains and started down the other side, we found the brakes had given out. Faster and faster we hurtled down the mountainside. Thomas opened the floorboards and worked on the brake system while O'Neal geared back and kept scraping the right front of the bus against the sheer vertical cliff to help slow us down. On our left was a sheer drop of several hundred feet.

Lieutenant Samuel Burns, present leader of our 2d Platoon, left the decision up to us. Did we want to stop the bus and get out? Or did we want to take the chance and try to keep up with the convoy?

It was unanimous; we voted to stay with the bus. "We'll make it," the men said. "No one's going to leave us behind."

Lieutenant Burns ordered us to "Stand up, hook up, and stand in the door."

These were orders given in preparation to jump from a C-47. O'Neal opened both doors. Half of the men stood in line at the front door, while the other half stood in line at the back door, ready to go out if and when O'Neal yelled that he couldn't hold the bus on the road.

I don't know what our chances would have been, jumping from a bus that was by turns rocketing down a mountainside and slamming into the sheer cliff to our right. But either would be better than going over the almost bottomless side to our left. We kidded each other about making a right or left front tumble when we jumped.

O'Neal worked at the controls until sweat ran freely down his body. All the while Thomas worked on the brakes. At times the brakes would work a little, then give out again. O'Neal kept easing the bus over to our right to catch the right front against the protruding rocks, each time making a terrible tearing and scraping sound, but slowing us down, then pull outward to pick up speed again. I think Thomas had the brakes working about the same time we hit the level ground of the valley.

Lieutenant Burns gave us the order to return to our seats as we rolled along in place with the rest of our convoy over fairly level ground.

We traveled through wooded hillsides, steep mountains with evidence of snow here and there, and through valleys and farmlands. After some miles over highways and back roads we finally came to the city of Meisbach.

As was the custom now, we did not hesitate to evict civilians from their homes and billet ourselves in the best available. Those who weren't on guard went from house to house looking for hidden weapons and legal loot, cameras, watches, binoculars, sausages from chimneys, and cold-storage eggs from cellars. All the food we brought to our kitchen to share with the platoon or company, while others showed off their newly acquired cameras and watches. I was never lucky enough to find either a camera or watch.

The next couple of days we gathered an array of vehicles that would make us look like anything but a victorious army. Parked on streets we had a convoy of anything that would roll, including vehicles that would not move under their own power. These we chained bumper to bumper to other trucks and buses to be towed by vehicles that would run.

A group of us were sitting at a large dining-room table in a large house, most of us writing short letters home to be sent off as soon as we established mail service. Someone, I don't know who, ran in yelling, "The war is over. The war is over. There's no more war. The war is over."

We went wild. The war was over and we had survived and would get to see home again. We broke out bottles of cognac, vodka, schnapps, and wine and drank as if alcohol were going out of style.

"Hooray, hooray, the war's over," yelled Brininstool, entering the house through a back window and waving his tommy gun. "Let's celebrate."

He fired a burst that splintered the top of the table and smashed a bottle of schnapps that stood in the center. We shot at the walls and ceilings, even tommy-gunned the elaborate cut-glass chandelier that hung over the center of the table. The rest of the squad was in the kitchen drinking cognac and frying goose eggs we had found hidden in a crock in the basement. This house must have belonged to a high Nazi Party member. The basement was filled with boxes upon boxes of clothing, shoes, and many other items not available even in the States during the war.

Bill Surface, or "Creepy," as we came to call him—his family owned two funeral homes in Roanoke, Virginia—stood over a hot wood-burning stove with a bottle of schnapps in one hand and a spatula in the other, frying goose eggs for one and all. We ate goose eggs, drank all sorts of drinks from every kind of bottle, and fired pistols and rifles at the walls and ceiling and threw grenades out through the windows. This was a celebration that would rival Normandy on D-day.

The next morning we all nursed big heads and splitting headaches. I found Carl Angelly sitting on the back porch wearing knee-high black leather riding boots with riding britches and a shirt embroidered with little flowers. He was drinking from a bottle that had flowers printed on the label.

"Have a drink—hair of the dog that bit you," he said.

I looked at the bottle. It was after-shave lotion I had seen in a bathroom medicine cabinet the day before. Carl looked disappointed when I told him. He threw the bottle away, saying, "That really wasn't bad stuff."

Then we learned that the war was not over, just a bad rumor. Orders came that we were to move out and to get rid of or destroy all vehicles we couldn't take with us, running or not. Our 506th Regiment had received direct orders from General Eisenhower that we were to liberate, or capture, Hitler's home, Berchtesgaden. This honor had been bestowed on our regiment for our combat record. The directive went out to all units to hold back, that we, the 506th, were to have the distinct honor of being the first to enter Berchtesgaden.

A German medical unit, complete with female nurses, had set up camp on the green near the center of town and were treating German military and civilians alike. We visited with them as we went through the city destroying with thermite grenades all vehicles that weren't in our convoy. Many of their badly wounded were receiving treatment in the open or in hastily set-up tents. We viewed them with detachment; it could have been one of us with the wounds.

As we returned from our duties of destroying vehicles, we met Brininstool standing at one of the large buses, holding a grenade in one hand. When I asked what he was doing he replied that he was going to set the thermite grenade on the engine and melt a hole through it. "The Krauts aren't going to use this one," he said. He pulled the pin, placed it on the engine, closed the hood, and walked away. The grenade went off. It wasn't a thermite grenade after all, but a white phosphorous grenade. A lot of the bits of burning phosphorous landed on Brininstool's head and arms. It was well that he had closed the hood, which contained most of the burning phosphorus; his wounds might have been fatal otherwise.

While Phillips and others rushed Brininstool into the house, to slow the white phosphorous from eating through his limbs by application of water, I ran to our aid station. They had no copper sulfate to put on his burns. *The Germans would have it,* I thought; many of those being treated here were victims of our shelling them with white phosphorus. I ran to their aid station and explained my needs to an English-speaking nurse. She handed me a tube of copper sulfate and gave me directions. We treated Brininstool with the ointment, which coated the particles, stopping the burning, and took him to our aid station, where they removed the white phosphorus and bandaged him properly. He would make the convoy trip with us.

Again we loaded into our vehicles, such as they were, and moved out, heading for Hitler's "Eagles Nest" in the Alps. On the highway we encountered hundreds, then thousands, of Germans streaming out of the hills to the highway—old men, young men, and men of middle age—all looking and calling to us to help them; they wanted to surrender. We knew they were probably hungry. Since their command had collapsed, how could they receive supplies, including food?

We weren't traveling that fast with our old vehicles and could call to them as we passed. Nearly every trooper in the convoy kept calling out, "The war's over. The war's over. Go to the rear." They in turn would ask, just where should they go? What should they do? Who should they report to?

We could only repeat over and over and point in the direction from which we had come and tell them, "Go to the rear. Someone will take care of you. Just go to the rear."

One group of Germans we came upon was coming out of the evergreen woods and down the hillside in a battle formation of skirmishers. There must have been at least a full division, perhaps more. They were fully armed, carrying rifles, machine guns, mortars, and *Panzerfausts*. (A *Panzerfaust* was a shaped-charge disposable rocket. It was armed, aimed, and fired at a target, usually a tank, and the tube thrown away. It was a one-shot deal and could not be reloaded.) The Germans had come to within about a hundred yards of the road edge off to our left. Most stopped and viewed with bewilderment the passing convoys of Americans, approximately fourteen thousand in our division alone.

Again we called to them that the war was over and, pointing back, told them to walk to the rear in the direction we had just come from. One gray-haired old German stood among a gathering of very young soldiers, his head partially bandaged. When he heard what we had said he threw his rifle to the ground, raised his hands, and said aloud in English, "Thank God. Thank God." We looked back. The younger men had thrown their weapons down where they stood and were following him down the road, back toward the rear.

We were on the autobahn again and finally rolling along at a good speed. We passed through Rosenheim, crossed the Inn River, and came to the large and beautiful Chiemsee. Here we pulled in alongside the water's edge for a relief break, and men could eat their K rations or smoked sausage and hard-boiled goose eggs, if any were left. Vetland had picked up an amphibious German Volkswagen jeep and was driving into and out of the water of the Chiemsee. Jackson pestered Vetland to let him drive—he wanted to take it into the water and cruise around, just to see how it felt. I don't believe there was too much in the way of lakes in the part of Texas where Jackson had come from. This would be quite an experience for him.

Finally Vetland said okay and let Jackson take it for a drive and a water trip. Jackson was like a kid, running all around the beach until he thought he had the feel for handling it, then easing it into the water, where he drove around in circles and figure eights. We were ordered to load up; we were moving out. Jackson wanted to try driving the Volkswagen up a steep bank instead of out on the level beach, just to see whether the small vehicle could take it or not.

He put it in gear, hit the bank, and gave it throttle. At first it seemed he would make it, but the bank was too steep. As the front of the jeep rose, the rear dropped; water filled the passenger compartment, and the little jeep slipped back underneath, leaving Jackson treading water. He finally made it to shore and had to face the wrath of Vetland. Jackson had sunk his toy, and we didn't have the time now to try and get it back. As far as I know it's still there.

We left the Chiem See, then turned off toward Siegsdorf. Just before coming to the town of Inzell we came up on the rear column of the French 2d Armored Division. A bridge had been blown out ahead and the French had no equipment with which to build a new span, so, there they sat.

It also happened that our regiment did have an engineer unit with us who had a Bailey bridge. These troopers moved forward to construct a way over the deep, yawning chasm that now blocked our way, using troops of our regiment as added labor. The French sat drinking wine, eating cheese, and watching. At this time a German heavy-caliber machine gun and a 40mm cannon opened up from a position high on the mountainside.

Everyone, including the French, dived for cover. Evidently the Germans on the hill hadn't worried about the French as long as they sat in place. But when we showed up with a bridge, the enemy opened up to keep us from crossing the chasm. The French began returning fire with the 50s mounted on their Sherman tanks. At the same time a group of troopers of the 506th climbed down the steep walls, crossed over at the bottom, and scaled up the opposite side. Climbing an almost vertical wall, they made their way to a point above the German gun emplacements and, using their rifles and deliberate aiming, killed the men on the gun crews. Descending to the enemy gun emplacements, they waved that all was in their hands and to go ahead with the bridge. These men remained in place to ensure other Germans wouldn't move in to take over the guns again. They would stay there until the bridge was complete and our columns had moved across.

Part of the French armored division now moved forward slowly, crowding the new bridge. All they were doing was bunching up, for the bridge wasn't complete as yet. Our drivers moved forward behind the French. A bad thing to do, bunching up. What if one lone German fighter plane showed up? There would have been hell to pay.

As we moved forward to the bridge site, the bodies of two German soldiers lay with their upper halves on the pavement, their feet on the shoulder of the road. Each French tank as it passed swerved so the right track passed over the bodies. From the waist up there was nothing but what appeared to be red jellylike hamburger smashed out along the pavement. We came to what was left of the bodies and skirted out around them. Someone had even stolen their boots. The French laughed to see us avoid running over the remains.

The bridge was going to take longer to build than had been figured, so we were ordered into Inzell, where we could bivouac in the houses of that town. At the same time, the 2d Battalion 506th was ordered back to the autobahn to circle farther around through Bad Reichenhall and enter Berchtesgaden from the other side.

Following military maps, the 2d Battalion 506th proceeded along their route until they came to another bridge that also had been blown out. After examining their maps they found they could still make it by a narrow dirt road, which they took, and continued on until they met with Maj. Gen. John W. O'Daniel, who, disregarding General Eisenhower's orders to allow the 506th Regiment to be the first to enter Berchtesgaden, ordered them stopped by his troops and would not allow them to pass. He wanted the honor to go to his own troops of the 3d Division.

Radio transmissions were made by the 506th Regiment's 2d Battalion to 101st command, telling of the problem with Major General O'Daniel blocking the way. It took time to send and receive orders to counter those of General O'Daniel. By that time the general had received word by radio that the 7th Regiment of his 3d Division had entered Berchtesgaden, and only then did he lift his roadblock and allow the 2d Battalion 506th to proceed.

In the meantime we had searched the German houses at Inzell and found many weapons, most of which were beautiful hunting firearms. Among them were Browning semiauto shotguns, over-and-under shotguns of high quality, rifles, drillings, and other weapons any one of us would love to own. There were also many antiques among the weapons, swords, daggers, and parts of armor. I found a Roman bronze short sword, which I felt would have some value to a collector, but we were ordered to destroy all weapons.

We stacked a goodly amount of TNT blocks in a pile, then placed all the ammo we could find for the firearms on top, ancient and modern, even powder horns and flasks of black powder. Finally we placed the firearms on the pile, some of the finest sporting firearms I have ever seen, lit the fuse, and took cover behind a large house. We produced a loud explosion and waited close to the wall of the house until all had settled. A rifle barrel came in a high arc, turning end over end, finally sticking muzzle-first into the ground about a hundred feet out in front of us. We didn't even bother to go look at it.

Word came that the Bailey bridge would take too long to complete, and that we should mount up and follow the same path taken earlier by the 2d Battalion. We made the trip back to Siegsdorf and onto the autobahn. Again we encountered many hundreds of Germans, all walking back the way we had come, most trying to make it well inside the American lines and as far from the Russian front as they could get.

Entering Bad Reichenhall, we were allowed to take billets. Our kitchen had set up in the open to prepare chow but was short of supplies. Second Squad took command of a large two-story house. Here we would stay until ordered to move on. Too many times had we been told that we wouldn't be in an area for more than an hour only to stay on for several days. We had to take what we could when we could.

As usual Angelly and I ran for the second floor, laying claim to a large bedroom with attached bath and large windows. I noticed there were no blackout blinds on any of the windows. Perhaps the war had never reached this far.

After settling in we found that we would be here at least until the following day. Justo Correa, Borchers, Angelly, and several others, including myself, went into the hills surrounding Bad Reichenhall to see if we could kill some of the deer we had heard were in this area. Spreading out, we worked our way up a hill toward the top ridge. Suddenly a bunch of large rabbits jumped up in front of us, heading up the hill. Two of our men appeared near the top edge, turning the rabbits back toward us. As one ran between Angelly and me I remarked on their large size and in that moment thought they must be the large European hares we had heard of. One of them had a rack of antlers. They weren't rabbits or hares, they were small deer, the largest about the size of a German shepherd dog.

We doubled back, jumping the deer again, or perhaps another herd, which once more headed toward the top of the ridge. I raised my M1 rifle and fired. A deer went down, then jumped back up, starting down the hill. Again I took aim and fired. The deer spun around, sat down on its rump, and slid downward. Again I fired; it went down. Three of us walked to the dying deer and couldn't believe its small size. I almost felt guilty, but we needed meat. The armor-piercing ammo we carried had gone through the deer without inflicting the immediate vital damage that a soft-nosed sporting load would have. That was the reason the deer were so hard to knock down and kill.

We hunted the rest of the afternoon and I killed seven deer. None of my buddies killed a single one. We carried them down the hills into town to our mess area, where the cooks were already in the process of butchering deer other troopers had brought in before us. The cooks took only the loins and hindquarters, the front legs and rib cage being too small to bother with. Altogether we had enough for a company chow and more.

Looting had carried on while we were hunting, yielding many Leica cameras along with other valuable items. Again I didn't get anything, for I had been out getting meat for the company. The large houses here were also filled with the finest clothing. The basements were crowded with large boxes crammed with expensive garments of all kinds, including women's fur coats. The only explanation we could come up with was that this was the clothing taken from wealthy Jews on their arrival at concentration camps before they were exterminated; the clothing then shipped to the homes of high-ranking Nazis.

We couldn't stay here. The 3d Division had usurped the honor that had been designated by General Eisenhower to be ours. Our 2d Battalion was traveling in a roundabout way to Berchtesgaden and was already ahead of us. The French were also ahead of us and they, too, were trying to be among the first to enter Berchtesgaden.

We boarded trucks and other vehicles and struck out again, heading for our last assigned goal, Hitler's home. Just outside Berchtesgaden our convoy came to a halt and we were ordered to dismount. We would march into Berchtesgaden on foot. Our troops formed up on either side of the road and we began walking, a mode of travel we were all too familiar with. We were assigned billets. Our 2d Squad was to be housed on the second floor of a building that contained a small museum on the first floor. We staked claim to beds and sleeping spots, dropped our packs and bedrolls, and, taking our weapons, went out to see to looting.

Others had entered Berchtesgaden long before us and had already gone through shops and homes and had made off with the cream of the looting crop. Elements of the 3d Division were already here. The French were also here ahead of us. Evidently our engineers had completed the Bailey bridge for them to use. And now we, of the three divisions that had raced to get here, entered last. But we did get to enter Berchtesgaden, Hitler's home. The rest having moved on, this was to be our assigned area to call home until ordered otherwise.

Things were moving fast and confusedly now. Here in Berchtesgaden General Tolsdorf was ready to make his stand and fight till the last man. His men called him "Tolsdorf the Mad" for his wild and reckless personal actions in combat. He had at times driven his motorcycle alone well behind the American lines on reconnaissance and had been wounded several times on his mad patrols. His division was one of the many that had confronted the 101st Airborne in the Battle for Bastogne and knew well what kind of troops we were.

Colonel Robert Sink sent a messenger, making contact with General Tolsdorf and asking him for a parley. The German general came with his aides and interpreters. When Colonel Sink asked him to surrender, the German general replied, "Damned if I will."

Colonel Bob, as we called Colonel Sink, laid it out pretty well to General Tolsdorf that we were here in Berchtesgaden as proof of the coming of Allied armies. In the end all of Tolsdorf's men would be either killed or wounded without just cause unless the general surrendered now. To fight on wasn't noble, it was foolish. It showed a disregard for the young men in his command who, but for him, might return home to mothers, wives, and sweethearts, and father healthy children with whom to repopulate Germany. General Tolsdorf had to reconsider. He did, and in the name of humanity surrendered his entire command to Col. Bob Sink and the 506th Regiment without firing a shot.

There were more Germans on the roads than we could count, but all we could do was start sending them to collective camps that in turn shuttled them back to Munich. We had camps of Germans now numbering in the thousands collecting in the open flatland of the valleys, where they made camp and pitched tents if they had them. We in turn tried to get them food supplies and establish sanitary facilities.

For the next couple of days we had life very easy. We roamed about the town looking for the big loot that we had heard rumors of. Where were all the riches the Nazis had taken from the countries they had plundered and dominated for so long?

Phillips, Angelly, and I entered the huge salt mines that were tunneled throughout the mountains around Berchtesgaden. The vaulted ceilings were so high that we had to crane our necks to look up at them. We wandered about the upper tunnels aimlessly but never found so much as a Reichsmark. It was impossible for us to go to the lower levels without the air pumps working, and since the Germans had sabotaged them before our arrival, we never did get to explore the lower tunnels.

Later, after our regiment had left Berchtesgaden, our engineers got the pumps going and other troopers found vast stores of art treasures along with gold and currency, totaling millions, in the lower-level tunnels.

Official word came out 8 May 1945 and rang down through the division. THE WAR WAS OVER. The war was over and we had survived. This time it was no false report. It was true, the war had really ended. How long until we would be returned home? We might as well live it up until that day came. What was important now was that the war was really over.

Back in our house after a hot chow—our mess halls had been established and we now had three hot meals a day—a couple of the men were playing guitars and singing while they sipped drinks from several bottles that stood lined up in front of them. Others of us were examining some very old weapons we had taken from the small museum downstairs. Most of the weapons, coins, and other objects we left in the neat glass cases, but a few of the weapons that caught our eye for one reason or another we took back to our billets with us. We had muzzle-loaders, broadswords, spears, lances, armor, breast-plates, a number of battle-axes, and an assortment of pistols, shields, and a number of the coins.

We buckled some of the armor onto ourselves (most of it being too small for our bodies) and with sword and battle-ax fought each other in mock battles. No harm was done to us, but the ancient armor and weapons were sorely used. We were amused that we were all too big for the armor, since I weighed 140 pounds, Phillips and Angelly about the same, and Leonard Benson was even slighter than we were.

None of these things interested Liddle. He didn't drink and old weapons were of no use to him; he was strictly interested in machinery or mechanical things, especially if they might be put to some use on his farm back in Utah. Liddle asked me several times to go with him down to a train we had seen sitting on a rail siding near the outskirts of town. All other troopers were looting in and around the homes and shops in the city, and the train on the siding was of no real interest. What caught Liddle's interest were the four German Me 109 fighter planes that were in open gondola cars just behind the engine. The wings had been taken off and stored beside the fuselages.

In our past talks we had both expressed our desire to learn to fly, and to own a plane ourselves someday, after we had returned to the States. "Maybe we can put one together and fly it," Liddle said, his eyes glistening with excitement.

"Okay, I'll help you," I said, "but you're not going to get me up in one of those things. It's hard enough to fly a plane over level ground with training, let alone up here in the Alps. And if you did get it up, someone would probably shoot you down. It is a German fighter, you know."

Phillips agreed to go with us, and together we walked down through town to the outskirts and approached the train. Most everyone else was too busy looking for legal loot to be bothered with a train engine and several forty-and-eight cars standing on a side rail. About the most popular prize men were picking up in their looting was a flat clam-style silver cigarette case with a map of Germany engraved on the cover and a small diamond set in place to represent Berlin.

Most of the hunt-and-search fever was dying down with slim pickings, and the men were now looking for other diversions, like drinking and women. It was against the rules to fraternize, but this was hard to enforce when GIs had been so long without female company and the German girls had had nearly all their men taken away in the service, many gone for years.

Liddle, Phillips, and I were surprised to find that Jerry Janes and two of his trooper buddies had arrived at the train just minutes before us. They had already climbed up to examine the ME 109s and were now wondering what was inside the forty-and-eights. Liddle and I climbed up on the forward gondola and began examining the German fighter planes; Phillips stood talking to Janes. Jerry and his two buddies had just forced the door of one of the boxcars and I had just eased down into the cockpit of a plane, feeling like a fighter pilot, when, after standing for long moments, one of Janes's buddies (I can't bring their names to mind) said aloud, "Gold."

We thought they were kidding, but the one man started rubbing something in the car and talking to himself. "Feel how smooth it is; it's almost slippery. It feels like butter. Feel how smooth."

Liddle and I climbed down from where we were and walked to the boxcar. The entire floor was covered with bars of pure gold. Jerry had already run to the next car and forced the door open. It, too, was filled with bars of gold. This couldn't be true. *Legal loot,* we thought. *It is legal to loot from an enemy country and this is all ours.*

A chill went through me; every nerve in my body quivered. We were rich beyond our wildest dreams.

Another car was opened. Against the back wall stood what appeared to be mail sacks. We climbed in and opened them. They were filled with money, American money all banded in small packets, mostly in twenty-dollar bills. This wasn't counterfeit; it was real American money, bag after bag of it.

Now it began to hit us. What were we going to do with it? How were we going to get it back home? If we started hauling it back to town, there would be a stampede that would run us over. We had to think of something. We stood talking for long minutes. Someone had the idea to haul the gold and currency up the hillside to one of the small abandoned salt mines, hide the money inside, and blast it shut. We could carry enough of the currency with each of us to live very well back in the United States, then in seven years we would all come back together, dig up the gold, smuggle it to Holland, fence it, and return home multimillionaires.

Holland was noted for diamonds. I would convert my share to diamonds; they would be easier to handle. As for bringing the diamonds into the United States, I figured it could be done with a private sailing vessel and a landfall on some unpopulated section of beach along our coastline.

We didn't think it was wrong for us to claim this legal loot, but at the same time we did want to keep it a secret and not throw the wealth away to several thousand other GIs. However, we had waited and talked too long, for evidently the *Bürgermeister* had knowledge of what was hidden in this train also. He must have had plans to get the money himself after things had quieted down. Now with our discovery the most he could hope for was to report it to the proper authorities and try to find favor in the eyes of the new military government.

He reported the treasure to our high command, and it wasn't long before General Taylor, Colonel Sink, and the *Bürgermeister,* along with jeeploads of officers and guards, were all around us. So intense was

our excitement that we hadn't noticed their arrival, especially the
one trooper who was still rubbing the gold and murmuring to himself how smooth it was. How slippery it was.

We were ordered to leave the place and not to touch anything.
Janes said, with all due respect, that this was legal loot and was rightfully ours; for the American money must have been accumulated
from independent sources, not like the art treasures taken from
other countries, which rightfully belonged to those countries. This
currency, if not the gold, should be ours.

"Not this time," we were told. "This goes to Uncle Sam. He'll de-
cide what to do with it."

We wandered back to our billets, sat down, and listened to the two
troopers still playing the guitars and singing. I picked up a bottle and
began to drink. We didn't tell the others of our find or how we had
been six of the richest troopers in the outfit for a very short time.
Later reports stated that eleven and a half million dollars in American money had been found on a train in Berchtesgaden and recovered, no names, no details. I do not recall a figure ever being released
on the amount of gold that was recovered from that train.

From time to time since, I have heard stories at our reunions and
such about several troopers who had found an immense fortune in
Berchtesgaden, had buried it, and were going back someday to dig
it up. Some of the troopers said they even thought of going back
themselves to wait for the looters to return. Amos West told me at a
reunion in Chicago in 1982 that he had had similar ideas of returning after seven years and waiting to see who showed up, but
never followed through. I told him the full story at that time and how
fruitless it would have been for anyone to return. There is not and
never was any buried Nazi treasure, not from our findings.

Phillips and I walked through Berchtesgaden a couple of days
later, just looking. Neither of us had found anything of value to liberate. There had been the 3d Division, the French Army, and the
2d Battalion of our own 506th looting through everything long before we came on the scene. We met Dale Jacoby and Floyd Smith,
who said they were on their way to Hitler's house and asked us to
come along. We agreed. The walk was long and uphill with patches
of snow on the way, but we finally arrived. I was greatly disap-

pointed. I thought we'd find a great large castlelike building. What we arrived at was a large house that had been bombed and stood in wreckage.

We made our way past the garage, which was on the lower right, and entered the front door at the top of a stone-and-concrete stairway. The floors were covered with debris and wreckage from the bombing; great holes had been blasted in the roof. We made our way to what I believe must have been the living room. It was large and spacious with a fireplace at one end. A window opening that seemed about twenty-five feet across looked out over the valley below with a view of the Alps all around, a beautiful sight. The window had been blown out, only the opening remaining.

This window, controlled by electric motors, had opened downward into the wall—the reason being that the sloped roof overhang was so close to the top of the window that there had been no room for it to open upward. We made our way through the building, which was all but empty. Scavengers and looters had taken all that wasn't nailed down. Even the chairs and tables were gone.

Men of all different units were wandering around sightseeing. A group of troopers sat on a brass bed in a large rear room drinking. We joined them for a drink of cognac and schnapps, then left. One of them claimed this very ornate brass bed was Hitler's personal bed. That didn't mean much to us at the moment. At this time there really was nothing of value left that we could carry with us, for men had even pried the treads from some of the stairs to carry away as souvenirs.

We left, returning to our billets, where I loaded up an old muzzle-loading shotgun and fired it out through an open window in our room. Since we had no way to carry all the old relics we had brought up from the museum downstairs, we carried them all back down, piling them on the display cases from which we had taken them. Let someone else put them back or take them as souvenirs.

Our unit left Berchtesgaden and moved into a small town named Lend, which was strategically located in a mountain pass through which enemy troops fleeing the Russians had to pass. Hundreds upon hundreds of Germans moved in convoys down through this pass, all calling to us, *"Mach schnell, mach schnell, Rooskies komen."*

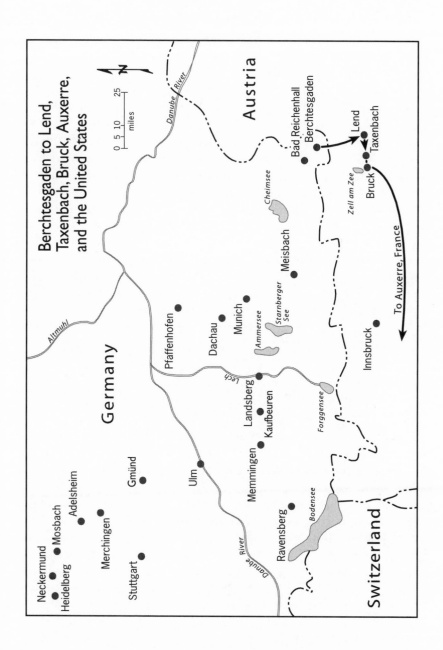

(Make fast, make fast, Russians are coming.) They all wanted to get well inside the American areas before the occupation zones were frozen and they would have to remain under Russian rule. *"Mach schnell, mach schnell, Rooskies komen."*

A tidal wave of Germans flooded into this narrow pass with its single road, all trying to make it into München (Munich) and freedom from the Russians and their retaliation. It became so congested that riots broke out, German fighting German, men and convoys trying to bypass each other. Our military had to set up roadblocks—in effect floodgates—in towns and cities all the way from the city of Munich back to the Russian front to allow only a manageable number of German troops at a time into Munich and from there into Germany proper. About a German division at a time was allowed to pass through Munich. When the way was clear in Munich another division would be allowed through from the next floodgate up the mountains from Munich, and so on back to us. Each time a German division would flow through, another two would pile up behind.

We at Lend were the first in the line of floodgates facing the Russian front and had to hold the Germans in check at this point until we received a call via military field phone that the way was clear to allow another division to pass through.

Here we disarmed the German troops, who were fully armed and ready to do battle with the Russians, or anyone else who tried to restrain them for too long. According to agreements made, the Germans were allowed to keep only one hundred rifles per battalion, thirty rounds of ammunition per rifle, and no automatic weapons. All their officers had to wear a white armband and each was allowed to keep a loaded sidearm. This was done so that officers would be able to maintain some control of their men. The officers chose the one hundred men who would keep a rifle and the thirty rounds.

As the German convoys pulled over to the roadside to make camp, we ordered them to come forward one company at a time and place their weapons in separate piles. One pile was of pistols, one of rifles, and the others were of automatic or heavier weapons, such as mortars or *Panzerfausts*. At the end of the first day we had a stack of pistols of all description well over six feet high and about twelve feet in diameter. Troopers constantly picked through this pile for choice Lugers, Walthers, Berettas, P-38s, old "Broomstick" models, Styers, and so on.

I took my turn as sergeant of the guard and placed four men at each end of town, where we could control the civilians coming and going and the DPs who were wandering in and out of convoys on their way to wherever. Curfew was set at 8:30 P.M., and no one, German soldier, civilian, or DP, was allowed out of quarters or on the streets after that time. I picked four Germans from a convoy who could speak English, two for each guard post on either end of town, to help with translating and other chores. I stayed at the uppermost guard post, where the disarming took place, and had the two Germans gather wood and build a large fire. It would be cold at night and we had to remain at post all through that cold night.

For long minutes we sat at the fire as night came on. I sat with my men to my left, the Germans to my right. No one spoke; it was sort of an uneasy time for both of us. Finally I spoke to one of the Germans, ordering him to fetch more wood. When he returned, the other German spoke to me for the first time. He was interested in our decorations, which we were required to wear now, and what outfit we represented. Both were shocked to learn that we were *Fallschirmjägers* (paratroopers). They had heard so much of us, most of it untrue: that we were all convicted murderers let out of jail to serve as paratroopers and that many of us had killed our own parents; these were the stories they were told.

As the night wore on, the two Germans loosened up and began to talk freely, expressing what they had been taught and how they felt. The one who did the most talking explained to us that it was all right to kill Polish people. The Polish were subhuman, and it was no crime to kill any of them whenever a true human wished to do so. He became caught up in his speech. The other sat listening but from time to time nodded in agreement. I was told that the evolutionary hierarchy started with the monkey, then the chimpanzee, the Negro, the Pole, the Russian, and finally culminated in the human being. All those below the white human being were classified as animals, and there should be no law or remorse against killing any one of them. I pointed to Chmeliewski, who was searching some Germans, and said, "There's a Polish-American paratrooper. Do you want to go over there and tell him that?"

The German looked as though I had thrown cold water on him. He sat straight upright on his log and said, "No, no, I don't want to tell him that. He would probably kill me."

"Yes, I think he would," I replied.

The two Germans looked around suspiciously. Then the one who had kept silent asked if we had any Indians in our outfit. "Yes," I replied, "we have Indians."

"No, not Indians like in India, I mean do you have any Americans Indians in your outfit; like 'woo, woo' Indians"—he gestured by grabbing his hair with one hand and making a slicing motion across his forehead with his other forefinger, as in scalping.

Again I replied yes, that we had several, all of them good fighters. They liked to use a knife, especially at night. Both Germans looked all around uneasily, got up, and put more wood on the fire. They kept constant watch into the darkness after that, neither of them getting drowsy. Several civilians entered our checkpoint, wanting to go on into Lend. I refused to let them go on. Our orders were that all civilians were to be inside by 8:30 P.M. If caught out after that they could be shot on sight. All those entering our checkpoint after curfew hour would be retained until daylight. All civilians were made aware of these rules, yet some openly chose to disregard them. All these civilians remained close to our fire but for some reason did not want to get too friendly with or close to the Germans from the Russian front.

As daylight broke the sun shone bright, and with it came another large convoy, all armed to the teeth. We stopped them and ordered them to pull to the side of the road. Most of the troops in the trucks didn't like that and began calling the familiar, *"Mach schnell, mach schnell, Rooskies komen."* We ordered them to be silent—they weren't going anywhere until I said they could go. Their divisional commander, a general of sorts—I couldn't tell one German rank from another—dismounted and strode confidently forward. He asked if I were an *Unteroffizier.* To which I replied that I was a sergeant and in command of this checkpoint.

The general was very polite and, eying me up and down with a slight smile, asked if he might be permitted to take his division on to Munich. His men, he explained, were tired and had fought well and long against the Russians. They feared they would be excluded from the western allies' lines and would suffer reprisals if left within the Russian lines. Now that the war was over their only wish was to go through Munich, to be processed, discharged, and return home.

I had to refuse the general, telling him that he could move his troops through only when I received word by telephone from down below that the roads were clear enough to allow troop movement again. The general wore a small .25-caliber pistol in a holster, which caught my eye, and I asked him for it. He refused, pointing to the white band he wore on his sleeve, and said that officers were allowed to carry a sidearm to control their troops. I asked what he expected to do against an angry mob of soldiers with a .25-caliber pistol, and I would really appreciate it as a souvenir. He smiled, turned, and went back to his troops, explaining the situation to his underofficers.

We had his troops dismount from the trucks and place their weapons on the growing piles of firearms and other weapons at the roadside. They all complied without a grumble. I believe they feared being stuck in a Russian zone so much, that they didn't want to cause trouble that might endanger their cause.

As it happened, the very moment the last German soldier had remounted his truck, the phone rang. The way was clear and I could allow the convoy to pass on. I went to the general standing by his vehicle with his officers and told him he was free to lead his convoy and division on through and should have no trouble with the roads all the way to Munich. He looked surprised, then quickly ordered the convoy to prepare to move out on his command. When all was ready he gave the command and they pulled onto the road, with his vehicle leading, and headed down the hills toward Munich. As he passed me sitting by the fire, I waved to him. He called back, *"Unteroffizier, hier,"* and tossed me the small Walther .25-caliber pistol in its holster. I stood, waved, and thanked him. I don't know if he thought that I might have had something to do with the approval for his convoy and division of war-weary soldiers to move onward. But whatever, I received a valuable souvenir: a Walther .25-caliber pistol from a German combat commanding general, retiring from the Russian front.

With each passing day our piles of liberated weapons grew. Word got around and soon convoys of jeeps hauling noncombat rear-echelon officers made daily pilgrimages from Munich to our checkpoint. Here they rooted through the mountainous pile of pistols, picking and choosing. Some took bags of them on their jeeps. I suspect they were selling them back in Munich.

Within days the great exodus of Germans fleeing the Russians slowed to a trickle and the number of DPs took a rise. More and more DPs began showing up, walking, riding bicycles, some with rickety old trucks, some of the trucks with makeshift cabin affairs built on the back.

One such truck pulled to a stop at our checkpoint while I was sergeant of guard. It contained two men, a teenage boy, and a woman who was sitting in the open rear of the cabin, or "caravan," as Europeans called it. The woman was humming and holding an infant child to her breast as though it were nursing. I checked out the men and the teenager; they were unarmed. Then the cab of the truck—no weapons. I had my men search through the caravan. All they had was clothing and some household utensils on board. Then I looked at the baby. It was dead. I called the DP men to the side of the caravan and told them the baby was dead and asked why the woman was trying to nurse it. They replied that she had given birth the day before and the infant had died this morning but she refused to admit it and kept trying to nurse it. They didn't have the heart to take the baby away and bury it alongside the road.

I asked the woman to let me see the infant. The younger man translated for me. The woman looked at me with eyes that seemed far away but she held the baby out for me to look at, without letting go. The baby was dead for sure and I told the woman so. She refused to admit it and clutched it back to her breast, trying to force the baby to feed. I ordered the family back into the truck and told them to go on through, with advice to the man who appeared to be the baby's father to bury the child as soon as possible. I watched them drive out of sight.

A couple of days later Borchers and I were standing on the bridge in Lend with nothing more to do than watch GIs and civilians go

about their business. We watched a crew of German civilians painting a factory. At that point they were busy on a large flume that ran
from the factory to a pair of tall smokestacks. I didn't pay much attention other than to observe that they were busy painting with pails
and brushes. Suddenly Borchers burst out laughing. "What the
hell's so funny?" I asked.

Borchers replied, wiping tears from his eyes, "They're painting the
building camouflage. The war is over. Why in hell are they camou-
flaging the factory?"

"They probably had their orders before the war ended and no one
has told them any different. You know how some of these Krauts are."

Company A moved again, this time to the town of Taxenbach. Furloughs were now being given out freely according to seniority. It was
here that a group of us walked to the river in our almost daily sport
of throwing empty schnapps and wine bottles in the water and
shooting at them with pistols as they swirled and bobbed in the fast-
moving current. I don't believe we ever hit one of them.

We met an SS man as he crossed a bridge from which we did most
of our shooting. He was tall, thin, and wore the traditional uniform
of knee-high black boots, black breeches and shirt, and a bashed-
down, short-visored cap. His cap, belt buckle, and shirt were deco-
rated with silver skull and crossbones. His shirt collar bore the
jagged twin lightning SS symbols. He wore a skull-and-crossbones
ring on one finger, a figure of a serpent wound in and around the
bones depicted on his ring.

He stood with his upper lip slightly curled back, looking down on
us, observing us for several long moments. We waited, waited to see
just what he would do or say. Having seen the concentration camps
on our way here and heard the reports from the inmates that most
of the savagery there had been perpetrated by the SS, each of us just
wanted an excuse to kill him. Finally he spoke to us, but spoke as
though we were nothing, that we were less than cattle.

He was interested in the trooper wings we wore on our jackets and
asked what they signified. We told him. Then he pointed at the long
rifle with the blue background of the Combat Infantryman's Badge
that some of us wore and asked what that was for. We could see in

his eyes that he was very impressed with the CIB and its long gun. Again we answered his question. His lip curled in a smug, half-held-back grin.

"We don't have such things in the German army," he said, as if our decorations were mere bits of worthless tin.

We asked him about his decorations, the skull-and-crossbones emblems on his uniform, and where and how he had fought. He began boasting, telling of the battles he had been in and the many deeds he and his comrades had accomplished. He pointed to a small ribbon tucked in at a buttonhole in the front breast part of his tunic and said very proudly, "Afrika, Afrika. My company fought in Afrika. All who fought there wear this ribbon to show this, that we fought in Afrika." He had pulled himself up to a stature of attention as he proudly pointed to the ribbon.

As we talked we gradually wandered to the center of the bridge that spanned the river that ran through Taxenbach. Here we stood watching the white foam on the rushing water as we listened to the SS man brag of his past and what it took to be an SS man. He told of wild parties, the torturous lessons and treatments given to Jews and the subhuman Poles. We listened, some of the men becoming so angry they could hardly restrain themselves.

The more he talked the more his eyes glistened as he told of battles and the killing of inmates in concentration camps. He felt it was right to kill or use subhumans any way he chose. I believe he thought that he was making an impression on us, but all the while we were raging inside with boiling hatred.

One of our troopers couldn't take it any longer. He stepped forward, yelling for the SS man to fight, fight with his fists and fight a man who wasn't a helpless prisoner. The German suddenly realized that he was in trouble, bad trouble. He refused to fight and tried to ease around us and head back toward the end of the bridge and land. We blocked his way. The SS man turned toward his challenger, begging not to fight. "Even if I win, your comrades will beat me."

We stood silent. He fell to his knees, begging not to be beaten.

"The war is over. Everything is true but I acted as a soldier. There was nothing wrong in what we did, We are soldiers; we followed orders."

Again the trooper challenged him but could not get the SS man to rise to the fight. Suddenly the trooper moved in, lashing out with both fists, beating the Nazi, who tried to cover his head and face with his arms. The trooper pummeled the hapless SS man until the Nazi lay unconscious on the deck of the bridge. Then he stooped and pulled the skull-and-crossbones ring from the SS man's finger and with his foot rolled him over the side into the swift water below, and he was gone from sight.

During our stay in Austria we captured several Nazi bigwigs, including Hermann Goering, Albert Kesselring, Robert Ley, Franz X, Schwarz and son, Julius Streicher, Karl Albert Oberg (the Butcher of Paris), and many others. We also had Paula Hitler Wolf, Hitler's sister, but released her after detaining her a couple of days.

Another Nazi captured was Erich Kempke, Hitler's personal chauffeur, who claimed to have witnessed the burning of Hitler and Eva Braun's bodies in Berlin. Eric had escaped through the Russian lines and made his way into Berchtesgaden.

In the meantime our engineers had repaired the sabotaged air pumps back in Berchtesgaden, allowing the troops who had relieved us there to enter the lower shafts and tunnels in the larger salt mines. There they recovered untold amounts of gold, silver, currency, and art treasures that had been looted from other countries. Famous paintings and statues were recovered, all of which could be identified and eventually would be returned to their rightful owners.

As squad leader I had a room with a large bed on the second floor of a house facing the valley below. The family who lived here was not put out but took up residence in the rear of the house, leaving the front entirely to our squad. We gave the lady of the house laundry soap, one cake at a time. She would cut the cake in half, one half for her family, the other half to do our laundry. Her teenage daughter made our beds and kept the rooms clean for whatever the men chose to give her out of their PX rations, chewing gum, candy bars, cigarettes for her father, and bath soap. Money no longer had an immediate value; it was the material goods that were sought after. Cigarettes for smoking or bartering were the top of the line, followed by chocolate bars, other candies, soap, sugar, and so on.

A couple of days after we had moved into Taxenbach, First Lieutenant Kennedy ordered me to choose several men and take them across the valley and up the hills on the other side, to a small village high in the mountains. If there were any German troops there, we were to tell them the war was over and order them to report in to our headquarters in town immediately. I chose Borchers, Angelly, Correa, Hull, Smith, and Jacoby, then went to the mess hall and asked the cook to make up enough lunches for each of us for two days; we would pick them up early the next morning.

We awoke long before daylight, put on our gear, took our weapons with two bandoliers of ammo each, Borchers carrying a tommy gun and several stick magazines, and went to the mess hall, where we had breakfast. We packed our lunches in our musette bags and left. We made our way down into the valley, crossed the swift-running river over a bridge, crossed the valley, and headed into the mountains. The road up was a fairly good one but steep. The higher we climbed, the narrower the road became, until at last we were a long way up and the road had become a footpath.

The footpath turned to a narrow ledge overlooking a long drop straight down; it must have been a couple of thousand feet to the bottom. Still we made our way. At last the path broadened again and finally the land itself broadened to a wide, rolling high ground where we saw a wooden fence.

We made our way through a gate in the fence and took up a worn path again, which led around to our right. As we made the bend we came to a group of about eight cabin homes side by side and facing each other with no real road between them, just a wide space with the grass worn down. Several German soldiers lounged around the front porch of one of the houses while one sat playing a guitar and singing.

When they saw us they didn't react at first. Then it must have dawned on them that we were Americans. They quickly grabbed their weapons. We froze in our tracks and I said to the others to leave their rifles at sling arms. I spoke to the Germans the best I knew how. *"Nein, nein, der Kreig ist kaput.* The war is over." I asked if any of them spoke English. They were confused. Here we were Americans in one of their remotest mountain hideaways and not attacking or making a move for our weapons. We moved forward. One of the Germans stuck his head inside the house and spoke, and a moment later another German appeared who apparently was an *Unteroffizier*. I asked if he spoke English; he replied that he did. I told him the war was over and we were here to notify them that they should go down to town and report to Munich, and then go home. The war was over.

His men were nervous and had their weapons in their hands but no longer pointed directly at us. They were listening intently. The sergeant conferred with his men, keeping an eye on us. I spoke again and said, "We knew you were up here. My whole division knows you're up here. That is why they sent us to tell you the war is over and for you to go down so you can go home. That is why we came to you without our weapons at the ready. How do you think we got here? We didn't get this far on our own. The whole American army is down in the valley." It was getting dark; the trip had taken us all day, starting before daylight. We could see movements of civilians sneaking peeks at us from doorways and windows, though none came out in the open.

The sergeant and men conferred a little more and finally agreed. They believed us. They would go down in the morning. I asked if we could spend the night here. The sergeant said yes, we can spend the night. "You sleep outside, we sleep inside."

We had no choice but to agree. We moved down near the wooden fence, ate our meal, and lay down to sleep. We didn't sleep much.

In the morning we walked back to the houses, said good-bye to the German soldiers without shaking hands, shouldered our weapons, and returned the way we had come without looking back. It was dark when we finally arrived at our billets. I made my report to the commander and went to bed.

I was one of the top in seniority of A Company men who had fought all the way through from Normandy till the present, and my name came up for furlough. Seniority men were visiting England, Switzerland, Paris, southern France, Scotland, and other places. Each of these furloughs would take a month or more. Time was added for travel from Austria, through France, and to the point where the trooper wanted his furlough to begin. I returned to England on my first furlough. The whole trip from beginning to end took a little more than a month. Besides money, we had to bring with us furlough papers, our PX ration cards, and extra food-ration coupons in case we stayed with civilian friends so that we could supply the food. Things were very tight in Europe for a long time after the war.

On returning from my trip to England I found our company had moved to the small town of Bruck, not too far from Zell am Zee and a little closer to Innsbruck. Zell am Zee was a large inland lake where we could go swimming and boating, and where on the Fourth of July we celebrated in style. An officer and several troopers made a parachute jump into the lake, to be picked up by waiting boats.

Our stay here became almost idyllic—little duty and a lot of time keeping an eye open for legal loot while enjoying recreation. The 1st Battalion Headquarters was stationed in Schloss Fischorn (Fischorn Castle), one of Hermann Goering's castle retreats that he had taken over as his own. It was here in Bruck that I obtained a small car that ran on wood. It had a little furnace installed through the trunk in which I would build a fire each morning just before breakfast. After breakfast I would bank the fire with wood and, by means of a battery-powered pump, siphon the gas from the smoldering wood in the furnace through the engine, start it up, and drive to Zell am Zee, Innsbruck, and all over the Alps. At times it required that we jump out and help push it over the highest peaks, but otherwise it ran like a clock—with no gas. At noon I would remove the ashes and stoke up the fire again for another four hours of driving.

I didn't do much while off duty except swim in Zell am Zee or ride horses that used to belong to the German cavalry and now belonged to the 101st Airborne Division. If there was excitement it usually came when I was on guard duty, as it did one evening when, again, I happened to be sergeant of the guard and Lieutenant Borrelli officer of the day.

I was sitting at a desk writing to my mother after darkness fell, and Lieutenant Borrelli was writing at his desk. We could hear singing, very low at first, then it swelled up through the valley. At first I thought someone had a radio on too loud. The singing became louder and louder. It was voices of many men and they were coming closer.

"Go out and see what that is," Lieutenant Borrelli told me.

I went out and could see far in the distance hundreds of torch-lights coming up the winding road of the valley. The singing grew, swelled, and receded. The valley carried the songs up to our ears; we could hear the ebb and flow of music for a couple of miles. I waited outside for a long time listening as the music got closer and the words became clearer. It was an army on the march. It was dark in the mountains and here was an army of German soldiers march-ing, singing. Their voices rose in blended chorus, filling the valley, their torches glittering like fireflies in the distance.

Soon lights in the houses came on, doors and windows were thrown open, women and girls crowded their porches and bal-conies, most in their night dress, not bothering to put street clothes on. They were laughing and waving, a joyous time for them; their men were coming home. Then the lead troops were in town, raising their voices as I have never heard men sing before. It amazed me at the time that they all knew the words and sang in practiced harmony.

I went inside to report to Lieutenant Borrelli. He said, "Go out and tell them to shut up."

I felt bad about that. I was enjoying the singing. I know they were the enemy, but that doesn't diminish good singing and that one could and should enjoy good singing.

Outside I met the commanding general walking at the head of a full division of German mountain troops, possibly nine to twelve thousand men. I faced him as seriously as I could and said, "My com-mander told me to tell you to shut up."

The German officer broke out laughing. When he got control he said, smiling, "Look, a full division coming home from the war. And look at all the beautiful ladies to welcome them. Do you really think I can tell them to shut up? No. If you want, you tell them."

I broke out laughing too. In the meantime the mountain troops kept marching and singing, all the while holding blazing torches high above their heads. It was an awesome sight, and the song was ringing in beautiful harmony through the mountain pass. This was a sight and sound I will never be able to forget. And how could these men, defeated in battle after warring since 1939, sing like victors? It was as though, for this night, they were victors, and their women knew it.

The general turned and strode to the head of his column, leading his men marching through the night. One could tell he was a soldier who took great pride in himself and his troops. Nearly an hour later the last of their members passed through our village, making their way toward the Brenner Pass and home. Long after the last torchlight had gone from sight the women stayed on to talk with each other. One by one they went in, closed their doors, and put out their lights.

Sergeant Conley Byrd, a replacement we had picked up after our Ruhr Valley campaign, along with Floyd Smith and many others, had a fancy for trains. In every town on our trips through Germany to Austria that was large enough to have a rail yard and trains, Sergeant Byrd would manage to get an engine running and run it up and down as far as the undamaged tracks would allow.

Now in Bruck he took over the electric-powered train and soon had it running from near the Russian lines clear down into Munich. Eventually he had a schedule that he kept almost to the minute, going through all the connecting towns. It came to the point where people—GIs, civilians, German soldiers, and DPs—came to depend on Byrd's train and its schedule. Every day at the appointed time in Bruck one could see masses of people arriving and waiting at the station for Byrd's train. They boarded without fare and carried loads of clothing and other personal belongings. They rode inside unless there was no room; then they rode on the tops of the cars, even with children. When General Taylor heard of this he made a special inspection, interviewed Sergeant Byrd, and made him the official operator, owner, and engineer of the railway and its equipment. What Sergeant Byrd said in regard to his train was law, superseding all rank other than that of General Taylor.

Immediately after arriving in Bruck we had ex-German soldiers build a dayroom for us where we had beer delivered from Munich every day on Sergeant Byrd's train. The dayroom was built at a cost of two American cigarettes per German carpenter per eight-hour day. It was also here that 1st Lt. William Kennedy, commander of Company A, received his captain's bars on his twenty-first birthday. A well-deserved tribute to a very young but very capable combat company commander.

Also at this time we were notified that a point system had been established for discharge. This seemed strange, since the war in the Pacific was still going strong and the Japanese mainland was yet to be invaded. There was talk around that it would take all the combat men on hand from both theaters to accomplish this feat. The high range of the system was eighty-five points. If a man had accumulated eighty-five points, he would be eligible for discharge and sent home. These points were accumulated at one for each month of service, an extra point for each month overseas, another point for each month in actual combat. And five points were awarded for each decoration; that is, Silver Star, Bronze Star, Purple Heart, Bronze Campaign Star, and so on. I counted up my points, which totaled ninety-three or more, most of them from combat time and decorations.

After thinking it over, I decided that I would rather stay in Europe a while longer. We were in no immediate danger here, and since I was one of the high men in seniority, furloughs were offered to me every time I returned from the one before. I felt that I had crawled up and down every ditch in Europe being shot at, and now I wanted to be able to tour and visit the countries I had fought in, and be able to walk upright through town. I was now twenty years old and there was no hurry to get back to the States.

This is where we stayed until we were relieved by the 42d Infantry, Rainbow Division, on 2 August 1945. The 101st shipped out in electric trains from 30 July 1945 to 1 August 1945 to the French border where we boarded the forty-and-eight boxcars again with the DDT spray and straw-covered floors, heading to Auxerre, France. Most of the rail tracks had been repaired, but still our train would slow to a walk, then speed up for a while. Along the way back we passed through Flanders Field, where small red poppies grew as a red carpet for miles over the farmland. An unforgettable sight recalling those who had died here during World War I.

# 9 Home

Arriving in France, the division was camped in three towns, Auxerre, Sens, and Joigny (pronounced Zhawny). The 1st Battalion 506th was stationed at Joigny in an old abandoned tenth century castle that had been converted years ago to a French cavalry post, then to a German prison camp during the German occupation of World War II, then to a U.S. airborne camp on our arrival. It was built on a high hill overlooking the town of Joigny. The River Yonne flowed through the center of the ancient city. Barges laden with coal and other goods were drawn up and down its length by horses walking along the banks.

Our high stone walls were breached by a large open entrance, floored by a flat-lying drawbridge that no longer worked. The walls encircled a number of buildings to make up an inner compound. Officers, naturally, had the large three-story building that dominated the courtyard. The mess hall, run by our cook, Him Lim, stood in the far right corner of the compound, while our latrines and wash area were set aside to the far left of all the buildings. A medic dispensary was located in the far left rear corner, while a room set aside for surgery and other more serious medical work was at the right of the front entrance. We of enlisted-man stock filled the stables in double-tiered bunk beds. Fifty five-gallon drums with the tops cut out to burn wood in were our source of heat. The stable roofs were high enough that the smoke went straight up and didn't cause too much discomfort.

The latrines took a little getting used to: a series of small holes lined in a row in the concrete floor with running water passing through and two elevated cement footprints to keep one's feet dry while squatting over the hole. Our wash area was the old stone-hewn

157

horse watering troughs of the long-ago cavalry. We washed our laundry in these troughs by hand and took baths the best way we could in the cold water. We did have a shower near the first aid building, but it was small and always crowded, so if one was in a hurry and not first in line, there were the cold-water horse troughs. All in all, we had had worse—and better.

Here we learned that we were now slated to go on to the Pacific without stopping in the States. The Allies would need every battle-experienced man they could muster to end the war down there. We would parachute on the Japanese mainland to spearhead that invasion, just as we had in Normandy. We were to spearhead the last and the largest of all invasions. Military strategists estimated that at least one million men would die on D-day Japan.

More new replacements came in to build our strength up to what it was before the Normandy invasion. Training picked up again. Day and night problems (which were training excercizes). Training new raw recruits we hoped would bring them in line with the old experienced combat men. A great many of these newcomers came in with rank—sergeants, corporals, and such—having transferred in from other existing infantry outfits. Many of our men who had been with the division from the beginning and had actually taken command of squads and platoons were long overdue for promotion. Now these promotions were denied unless the newcomers would voluntarily take a demotion to private. None of the new men were willing.

This caused hard feelings among the older men denied rank. "To hell with the new men. Why should we train them and teach them how to stay alive when they won't do anything for us? Let them learn the hard way, or die. Why should a seniority man with combat experience follow a green, inexperienced noncom into combat and take his orders?" This was the feeling of nearly all the older men who were denied promotion because of an overload of new replacements with rank. The feeling was that all our command had to do was to demote the newcomers with a broad stroke of the pen and give rank where it was due and where it would do the most good when we next went into combat. The command refused to act and so did many of the older men; the new noncoms received little or no cooperation from any of the older combat-experienced men.

On a night problem I was to be machine gunner. Bill Surface, our last gunner, had shipped home on points. I had more points than he did and now I was beginning to wish that I had shipped home also. We walked down a dark, lonely French country road to get in position to outflank an enemy that was dug in, in a wooded area a couple of miles up ahead. I had "gutted the gun," in order to make it lighter. After all, we weren't going to be doing any firing; this was strictly a dry run. "Gutting the gun" meant removing the barrel and the heavy machined bolt, about half the total weight of the forty-two-pound gun, and carrying just the housing and barrel jacket. Who would know the difference?

After we had traveled a way, Captain Kennedy moved in alongside me and in a low voice said. "Burgett, the next time you gut the gun, put a broomstick in the barrel jacket. The moonlight is shining through." I thought I was outfoxing the man who probably invented "gutting the gun."

Our training continued with more night and day problems, double-timing, and checking our weapons out on the firing range. Ordnance trucks came into our compound to work on our personal and crew-served weapons, replacing worn parts and in general getting all in readiness for a sustained tour of combat.

I had a reoccurrence of trench mouth, an infectious disease that I had originally contracted while in a long stay of combat in Holland under General Monty. I'd had a small bout with the same thing in Austria, and now again in France. I was sent to the hospital in Joigny, where another trooper had the same malady. A doctor came in telling us that he had what he thought was a cure for trench mouth and we were "volunteered" for an experiment. To refuse an order meant a court-martial. The doctor prepared and injected a hypodermic in a vein in our arms. This went on for three days. It didn't work. "Well, back to the lab," the doctor said. "Looks like we'll have to use the old standby, penicillin."

I didn't know the other trooper, but as we took the penicillin treatments we talked of the invasion of Japan and of our chances of surviving another invasion. A "ward boy," as they are called in the military, came in and recognized me as having been in the same jump class with him in Fort Benning back in 1943. He recalled the plane I was supposed to have been in when it crashed and burned, killing all of the men I'd been scheduled to jump with that night. Only a fractured leg I'd received on my first jump had saved me from that death.

The next afternoon, after another penicillin shot, the ward boy (I can't recall his name) hurried into our ward. "Did you hear the news?" he said. "The war is over. They dropped some kind of a bomb in Japan that wiped out a whole city."

I couldn't believe it. "No way," I said. I had been in bombings and artillery bombardments and I knew that no one bomb could wipe out an entire city. I thought he was just telling us that because he knew we were all scheduled to make the big drop in Japan.

"It's true," he said, "one bomb wiped out an entire city. It came over the radio not too long ago. The war is over."

Still skeptical, I asked, "Just how big was this bomb?"

He replied, "They say it was the same size and shape as a football."

Now I knew he was kidding or just didn't know what he was talking about. Probably he'd misunderstood someone's try at outlandish propaganda.

Again he tried to convince us. "I don't know what was in it. They got some new kind of stuff, and that one bomb the same size and shape of a football destroyed an entire city and the war is over."

The other trooper and I went to another ward on the same floor, asking the patients there if they had heard the news. They confirmed it. A bomb had been dropped, a city was wiped out, and Japan had surrendered. The war was over.

"Sick or not," I said, "I'm going to celebrate. I'm going out and have a few drinks." I had some money and asked the men in that ward if they would like to come along. We could have a few drinks, I would buy, and we would all be back before anyone would miss us. They all declined. My companion said he didn't want to take the chance, he had already been caught AWOL. "You can't get out anyway," one of the men in the ward said. "The uniforms are all locked up in the closet there in the corner."

I found the ward boy and asked in the name of friendship and the old class in jump school if he would get me the key for the wardrobe holding the uniforms. He did. I returned to the ward with the key and, to the amazement of the men in the room, unlocked the door. The wardrobe was filled with field grade uniforms and two enlisted men's uniforms. One was mine, with three stripes on the sleeves. "Kee-riste," I said. "There sure is one hell of a lot of brass in here." One of the men in the room asked where I had gotten the key. "That's a military secret." I replied. I took my uniform and left, locking the wardrobe behind me and returning the key to the ward boy.

I met with another trooper in town and together we went to a bar, where we shared a bottle of wine I had purchased. We drank while we discussed the unbelievable turn of events, the destruction of a city with one single bomb, and such a small bomb at that. We didn't get drunk; we just wanted a release and a couple of drinks to celebrate the end of the war. Now I recall at every anniversary: I was in a hospital with trench mouth in Joigny, France, when Hiroshima was bombed with the first atomic weapon in history.

I returned to the ward early, much to the surprise of the patients there, unlocked the closet, put my uniform back, locked the door, returned the key, and went to bed. And slept. I learned a little later from the ward boy that the patients I had invited out to have a drink with me were the field grade officers to whom the uniforms in the closet belonged.

The war with Japan was over. I could scarcely believe it. Our mission was canceled; we were to go home instead. Go home to America. America—it seemed to be only a dream now, a misty wonderland that had existed only in our minds.

After being released from the hospital, cured, I returned to duty. The training didn't let up. Then I was scheduled for another furlough, but before the furlough we were told that our time was up to make another jump. We had to make at least one jump every three months to keep our jump pay. This jump wasn't mandatory, but if we refused, we would be taken off of jump status and would receive no extra money. We all agreed that we had come into the military as paratroopers and we would all go out as paratroopers. We would make the jump and keep our pay. We loaded on trucks, which took us to an airstrip in a large grassy field a short way out of Joigny. There we drew parachutes from the back of a six-by-six truck and harnessed up. Joseph Nardi, Dobrich, Smith, Hull, Surface, Phillips, and all the others climbed aboard a C-47, 18 September 1945, 2:30 P.M.. The plane climbed to more than fifteen hundred feet, the highest altitude we had ever jumped from except for possibly our jump in Holland. A glorious cool fall day, the sun shining bright. "The descent is good in the cooler air," Nardi called to me. I turned and waved and he snapped my picture with a camera he had readied before our jump.

We guided our chutes toward a group of trucks on the ground. We landed and unbuckled our harnesses, rolled up our chutes, and made our way to the trucks. Our cook, Him Lim, had a table set up at the tailgate with hot chocolate and doughnuts. We hadn't had it this good in Normandy.

Several days later I was issued an extended pass to Paris. Bill Rary, a private in my squad, was somehow now the first sergeant. I was alone; many of the higher-pointers had shipped out. I met two other troopers in Paris whom I hadn't known before, but these men were game for anything and fun to be with. For two weeks we did whatever young twenty-year-old single men just out of combat with a lot of money do in Paris. We were young and we were alive. Several days after our furlough time had run out I managed a phone call back to the base by going through our code name of "Kangaroo," the 101st Airborne Division; to "Kidnap," the 506th Regiment; to "Red," the 1st Battalion, and asked if the division was still there. A voice said, "Why don't you come back and find out?" and hung up. It didn't sound good, and the three of us caught a train to Joigny. The two other men went their way and I walked up the hill and through the main gate. Most of the men were gone. Beds and straw mattresses were being burned in the courtyard. I found all the old combat men in the division had shipped out for the States and home. Liddle, Benson, Phillips, Angelly, Brininstool, Jerry Janes, all the old men, all of my close buddies I had gone through so much with, were gone. Not only that, but to add insult to injury, I was told I was off of jump status. The whole division was being taken off jump pay. We had made the required jump 18 September 1945 to ensure we would stay on jump status until discharged, and now our government and our command had reneged. I was told that while we were in transit we would be off jump pay. That was a directive.

The old castle was only half full of men. Now that the war was over, all those who qualified under the point system had shipped out for the States and discharge. I found myself among new and strange faces of late replacements fresh from the States. They looked in awe at my decorations, my bronze arrowheads for invasions and the campaign stars on my ETO ribbon. I was an old man. I felt like a misfit, an old man among kids.

That night, in a small bar in Joigny marked "Off Limits," I sat alone drinking wine. I could go home now. I raised my glass. "Here's to the last one. Here's to the next one. Here's to the ones we left behind."

# Epilogue

The Nazi war machine had finally been crushed, but only after years of total war, a tremendous cost in human lives, suffering, and the loss of property. The war had been long, hard, and brutal. More than forty million people in the world had died as a direct result of World War II, and thousands of others had been crippled in body and mind. Cities, towns, and villages had been ravaged and leveled, and families scattered, many never again to be reunited. Mass graves holding the remains of bodies that once had housed human souls lay hidden in secret places. The war in Europe had come to an end.

Once again people could walk the streets of Europe without having to scuttle from one protection to another and hide in darkened cellars like animals. Cities and towns were beginning to be rebuilt, blackout curtains were removed, lights, for the first time in years, glared brazenly out into the night. Streetlights that still existed shone brightly where they had been blacked out since before 1939. As one very young Londoner exclaimed when he stepped from home with his mother one night, viewing, in wide-eyed amazement, lighted streetlights for the first time in his life, "Mommy, look, the stars came down from heaven."

The war had indeed ended in Europe, but much work still lay ahead. An army of occupation had to be installed to oversee a warlike people who had willingly joined with their Führer in the destructive conquest and enslavement of their neighbors.

We, the 101st Airborne Division, along with other combat divisions, became the logical choice to become the army of occupation.

Combat men would take no guff from the enemy. They would lean hard on any troublemakers and former Nazis, military or civilian, if they chose to create trouble. At the same time it seemed unjust to force men who had served in combat for so long, and had managed to stay alive despite their hardships and wounds, to take the added burden of policing the ones they had conquered. These men should rightfully be allowed to return home first, as recompense for their hardships and reward for their longevity in combat.

The system that was established would allow the veteran with a minimum of eighty-five points to choose whether he wanted to return home, take a discharge overseas, or reenlist overseas. I was surprised that several troopers took their discharge immediately while others reenlisted. Those who reenlisted were discharged before an officer and sworn back in immediately while standing in the same spot.

A great shuffling of troops in the airborne divisions began to move high-pointers into seniority groups and low-pointers and new replacements into army-of-occupation and combat-ready divisions. Many high- and low-point 101st and 82d Division men found themselves transferred not just to other battalions and regiments, but to other divisions as well—a blow to the morale of men who had served in combat and shared camaraderie, danger, and death in one division, only to be torn away to serve the last days among strangers in an entirely different division.

After leaving Berchtesgaden, A Company alternately billeted in Lend, Taxenbach, and finally Bruck, Austria, not too far from Innsbruck. Our duties were to perform as the army of occupation, act in capacity as General Eisenhower's appointed honor guard, and in between relax and do some sightseeing in and around our areas. The oldest seniority men were granted furloughs to places of their choice in Europe. As one of the high-seniority men I took trips to England, Scotland, Switzerland, southern France, and Paris. On returning from these various furloughs I would find my company had changed residence to another town or city and more of the "older" men had shipped out for home.

The 101st Division entrained 30 July 1945 to 1 August 1945 and shipped from the Bavarian Alps in fast smooth-running electric-powered trains, leaving behind fairly modern cities and towns with running water and warm clean homes in which we had billeted the past several months. On entering France we were switched to older trains drawn by slow-moving, coal-burning, antiquated steam engines that belched steam as a cloud from a multitude of ruptures in the boiler and pipes.

The sad state of transportation in France, and of French life in general, was a result of years of plunder and deprivation under the Nazis, while the Bavarians and many other Alpine Germans went virtually untouched by the war. Days later we arrived in the area of Auxerre, Sens, and Joigny, France, where the 101st Screaming Eagle would make its new home until further orders.

The 82d was to head home from France immediately with all high-pointers from the 101st and the 82d Divisions, discharge those high-pointers, and be inactivated. The 101st would take on all low-pointers and stay on as a regular army airborne division and make the big victory parade in New York City; a fitting honor for a much-decorated division.

Again orders were changed. The 82d was to proceed immediately to the States, where the high-pointers would be discharged and the division remain active, while the 101st was to be inactivated as soon as possible. With a stroke of a pen and no formal ceremonies, speeches, or fond good-byes the 101st Airborne Division was inactivated in France, 30 November 1945. An inglorious end to one of the finest fighting divisions ever to be assembled in the world.

A few other paratroopers such as myself returning from lengthy furloughs found ourselves among newly arrived untested GIs who stared at us as curiosities, and in wonder. We were then notified that while the division was in transit we would be off jump status and receive no jump pay. We felt betrayed. We were loners in what was left of our Screaming Eagle Division. That evening as I was drinking wine in a bar in Joigny, I decided it was time to go home. My group, all unknown to me, sailed for the States 14 December 1945, landing in New York Christmas Eve. We were not allowed to remain on deck that evening to view the big city and all the lights but were confined by order belowdecks until Christmas morning, when we disembarked. On our trip home aboard a Liberty ship we were reminded that we had been stripped of our jump status and jump pay even though we had voluntarily made the last required jump. Still we were paratroopers, proud men of the 101st Screaming Eagle Division. We had kept the "rendezvous with destiny" Gen. Bill Lee had promised, and we, the men, had given the 101st Airborne a history.

After fighting through four major campaigns and being wounded three different times I was discharged from the military at the age of twenty. I could not vote, buy a car on contract, or buy a beer. I was not legally old enough. I returned home the first of January 1946 to care for my mother, working at one job then another until she remarried. I could not stand still. I had to do something, but I didn't know what; at times I felt as though I was going to explode, or fizzle away to nothing.

I took flight lessons and became a licensed pilot in 1947, then traveled to California, where I bought a sailboat and a plane, a "Timms" plywood-built, two-place, open-cockpit low-wing, and took extended flight training. After selling my plane I bought a surplus jeep and traveled through many of the states, but did not hold any job for more than weeks or months at the most. I gained vast and varied experiences in many phases of life and work over the years, but lacked a formal high-school diploma.

At twenty-seven I returned home to Michigan and met the girl who eventually became my wife, Twyla Moonen Austin. I fathered four sons, Kenneth, Mark, Gary, and Jeffrey, and one daughter, René. Even then I could not bring myself to remain long with one job. In the end, however, I did return to carpentry, retiring at sixty-two as a licensed homebuilder to take up writing and put on record my memoirs of my comrades, my division, and our actions. Twyla and I have been married forty-nine years at the time of this writing and have nine grandchildren and nine great-grandchildren. Over the years few, if any, of my combat comrades have ever been in trouble, even to the point of getting a traffic ticket. During the time of carpentry and raising a family I attended Brighton High night school for two years in Brighton, Michigan, and in June 1972 received my high school diploma from that school—something I had always wanted.

There has never been, and is not yet, one hour of any given day or night of my life that I have not thought of or had dreams of combat and my comrades. Combat, or war, has been with me since I was nineteen years old and will be with me until my last breath.

Some ask, "How can you remember all that you have written about?" I answer, "How can I forget?"